Developing Literacy Skills in the Early Years

A Practical Guide

Hilary White is a freelance writer and educational consultant living in Somerset. She has a BA Hons in English Literature from Bristol University and a PGCE from Redland College. She has taught in both the primary and the nursery sectors and lectured for many years at an early years training college. She has written a number of books in the fields of creative development and communication, language and literacy and is a regular contributor to various early years publications. She has a particular interest in the picture book and has spent a number of years researching its role in the young child's learning and development.

Developing Literacy Skills in the Early Years

A Practical Guide

Hilary White

P·C·P

Paul Chapman
Publishing

Paul Chapman Publishing
A SAGE Publications Company
1 Oliver's Yard
55 City Road
London EC1Y 1SP

SAGE Publications Inc
2455 Teller Road
Thousand Oaks, California 91320

SAGE Publications India Pvt Ltd
B-42, Panchsheel Enclave
Post Box 4109
New Delhi 110 017

Library of Congress Control Number: 2004 116 991

A catalogue record for this book is available from the British Library

ISBN 1-4129-1023-4
ISBN 1-4129-1024-2 (pbk)

Typeset by Pantek Arts Ltd, Maidstone, Kent
Printed in Great Britain by Cromwell Press, Trowbridge, Wilts

*To Stephanie Shimmin and the children of the
Maria Montessori Nursery School, Ealing
Deborah Wring
Ricky Sanderson
My family: Michael, Joe and Hannah White.*

With grateful thanks for all their help and support.

Contents

How to Use this Book

Introduction

This book focuses on literacy development during the all-important Foundation Stage years. It is aimed at anyone who works with the three-plus age group – nursery nurses, nursery teachers, Reception class teachers, nursery and Reception assistants and students practising in day nurseries, nursery schools or Reception classes.

The book sets out to offer a wide range of practical activities that can be used to help children develop the skills of reading and writing. The chapters break up the field of literacy development into six broad areas. Chapter 1 looks at organizing a literate play environment and working with groups; Chapter 2 covers the sounds of spoken language; Chapter 3 the association between sounds and letters; Chapters 4 and 5 focus on early writing and reading experiences; and Chapter 6 looks at the role of the picture book. The final chapter, Chapter 7, provides information on planning, assessment and recording, showing how each activity links with the *Curriculum Guidance for the Foundation Stage* (QCA, 2000) and the 'Reception' section of *The National Literacy Strategy: Framework for Teaching* (DfEE, 1998).

The chapters and activities are, to some extent, placed in a chronological sequence. For example, the process of exploring the sounds of language (Chapter 2) should be started before introducing the symbols that represent those sounds (Chapter 3). However, young children do not necessarily learn in a linear fashion and it is important to remember that many literacy skills develop side by side. Introducing letters (Chapter 3) will overlap with many of the sound exploration activities in Chapter 2. Early writing and reading experiences in Chapters 4 and 5 have been separated to help facilitate planning, but in practice, these skills are inextricably linked. Likewise, although linking sounds and letters (Chapter 3) and recognizing common letter clusters and words as a whole (Chapters 5 and 6) are dealt with in separate chapters, they all come under the umbrella of 'absorbing printed language'. Perhaps most important of all, although **The Role of the Picture Book** is the final activities chapter (Chapter 6), children should be introduced to the book corner and picture book related activities as soon as they arrive in your setting. Where it is necessary that activities should follow each other in order to build up skills, this is emphasized in the **Readiness** section attached to each activity.

Overall, the book has been designed to be 'dipped' into, and many of the activities constitute different ways of exploring the same skill. The games and activities are also designed to be fun and varied. This is an age group that needs to be on the move and utilizing all five senses to explore the environment. Many of the activities encourage the child to be active, both within the group and within the setting. Wherever possible, activities are based on familiar rhymes, stories and objects, providing a meaningful context for learning.

Although a number of the activities are quite structured and adult led, it is important to remember that play should be at the core of the child's literacy experience. Many of the activities have strong play elements – playing with alliteration, playing with writing materials, playing with story props – and it is important to exploit any play opportunities that might emerge from an activity. Equally important is the setting up of a play environment to support the development of literacy in all its many aspects. For more information on encouraging literacy related play, see Chapter 1 (**The Setting**).

Each activity or group of activities is presented in a similar format, to help the reader access the information quickly and efficiently. Most of the activities are explained in detail and, where appropriate, the activity descriptions and **Tips** sections include suggestions for differentiation (meeting the needs of a range of abilities and ages) and inclusion (catering for children with additional needs). The activities also include the following headings:

- ■ **Resources:** a list of resources is given where relevant. At the end of each chapter, the **Useful resources** section recommends items that can be purchased.

- ■ **Tips:** practical little suggestions designed to extend the activity or help it run more smoothly. This section also includes suggestions for linking an activity with a particular topic, story or role play.

- ■ **Readiness:** guidance as to what a child needs to be able to do, prior to joining in an activity. Specific ages have deliberately not been given, as rates of development vary so much from child to child. Always choose activities based on what a child is ready for, rather than age alone, and never push the children beyond the limits of their willingness or capability.

- ■ **Curriculum guidance:** a list of relevant Stepping Stones and Early Learning Goals (QCA, 2000) and linked statements from *The National Literacy Strategy* (DfEE, 1998). The activities aim to cover every Stepping Stone in the 'Linking sounds and letters', 'Reading', 'Writing' and 'Handwriting' Early Learning Goals.

The activities explained

This section looks at each of the activities chapters in turn and explains their theoretical underpinning, the purpose of the activities and how they can help the child's overall literacy development.

2

Chapter 2: The Sounds of Language

Chapter 2 focuses on the development of phonological awareness. Phonological awareness is the ability to tune in to and identify the sounds that make up our language. Until quite recently, phonics was taught from grapheme to phoneme. In other words, children were given the letter symbol and then learnt the sound it represented. *The National Literacy Strategy* now recommends that children should be given the opportunity to explore the sounds that make up a word, before being taught the graphemes that represent that word. This approach makes good sense, given that children have been experiencing oral language from birth if not before.

Apart from all this experience of the spoken word, young children have a natural sensitivity to the rhythms and patterns of spoken language. This is something we can exploit to good purpose in the early years setting with lots of activities designed to explore rhythm, rhyme and the individual phonemes that make up our language. The chapter is divided into three sections – **Rhythm and rhyme**, **Initial sounds** and **Segmenting words**.

Rhythm and rhyme

There is an indisputable link between rhythmic activities and early literacy success. For example, the strong rhythm of a nursery rhyme breaks words into their component syllables – so the child automatically hears *hickory dickory* as *hick-or-y-dick-or-y* when singing or reciting the rhyme. This ability to segment words is particularly important to the writing element of literacy development. Clapping out the rhythms of language is a great way to introduce the rhythms of spoken language, and ***Clapping names***, ***Clapping rhymes*** and ***Clapping words*** are quick, easy and fun to do.

Being able to detect rhyme is another direct step towards the more refined skill of breaking a word into its onset (initial sound) and rime (the end unit that produces the rhyme); for example, *J-ill / h-ill*. The ***Playing with rhyme*** activities highlight rime by encouraging children to identify and explore rhyming words, as well as enabling them to be creative with language.

Most important of all, the activities in this section help children to discover the pleasure to be gained from rhythm and rhyme – an important precursor to enjoying both poetry and music in later life.

Initial sounds

Listening for the initial sound of a word is the first step in the process of detecting the individual phonemes that make up that word. It is important that children have lots of experience with the rhythms of multisyllabic words and nursery rhymes, as a prelude to exploring initial sounds. They also need to have developed both their listening skills and an awareness of syllables, before being expected to listen out for individual sounds. Alliteration is useful for highlighting a particular sound for the ear to pick up. Alliteration occurs where a phrase or sentence contains more than one word beginning with the same sound. Many traditional rhymes use alliteration; for example, *Lucy Locket*, **Baa,**

Baa, Black Sheep. The **Playing with alliteration** activities draw on nursery rhymes and strings of alliterative words to help children focus on a given sound.

If children are to be successful in 'sounding out' words for later reading and writing, it is essential that they learn correct pronunciation for the individual phonemes. Check that your own articulation is accurate (see Warland, 2004) and keep reiterating correct pronunciation as you explore the sounds of language with the children. Learning to listen out for, identify and pronounce individual phonemes is a long process that needs lots of practice. Play alliterative games, *I spy* and activities such as the **Initial sound games** to provide practice and reinforcement. If we can lay strong foundations when it comes to detecting initial sounds, the later process of sounding out a word will come much more easily to the child.

Segmenting words

Once children have had some experience in identifying initial sounds, you can introduce the process of listening for the other phonemes that make up a word. This involves identifying the initial, middle and end sounds of a simple consonant-vowel-consonant (CVC) word such as *mat* (*m-a-t*) or *cup* (*c-u-p*). As with initial sounds, *I spy* makes a useful (and by now familiar) format for introducing all the sounds that make up a word. Remember that the focus is on 'sound' rather than 'spelling'. In other words, if you want to sound out *head*, you will end up articulating exactly the same middle and end phonemes as with the word *bed* – even though the middle phoneme for *head* is represented by the grapheme *ea*, while the middle phoneme for *bed* is represented by the grapheme *e*.

When introducing children to the **Segmenting words** activities, start off with simple, phonetically regular words. The *Curriculum Guidance for the Foundation Stage* (QCA, 2000) states that, by the end of the Foundation Stage, children should be able to 'hear and say initial and final sounds in words and short vowel sounds within words' – for example, *a* as in *hat*, or *e* as in *leg*. The Department for Education and Skills (DfES) guidance *Playing with Sounds* (DfES, 2004) also suggests introducing graphemes/phonemes in staged groups. These groups are based on 'usefulness, ease of discrimination and development of handwriting' and they include some of the most common double graphemes and consonant blends:

- ■ Group 1: s m c t g p a o
- ■ Group 2: r l d b f h i u
- ■ Group 3: v w y z j n k e
- ■ Group 4: ll (*hill*) ss (*kiss*) ff (*cuff*) zz (*buzz*)
- ■ Group 5: sh ch th wh
- ■ Group 6: ck (*duck*) ng (*ring*) qu (*queen*) x (*fox*).

For settings who are following this guidance, choose letters, words, objects and pictures to fit into these groupings. For example – Group 1: *cat, pot, mop, cap, Sam*; Groups 1 and 2: *hat, dog, cup, pig, log*; Groups 1, 2 and 3: *web, van, zip, red, jam*; Groups 4, 5 and 6: *Bill, hiss, fish, chick, singing*.

Although the focus in this chapter is on the sounds of language, it is essential that segmenting words is looked upon as preparation for becoming a writer. The children should be offered a seamless progression from *sounding out* the phonemes in words to the *writing* process of representing those phonemes with graphemes. This means that the **Segmenting words** activities in this chapter should lead directly on to activities such as **The word basket** in Chapter 4 (**Becoming a Writer**).

As with all activities in the early years setting, a positive experience is the most important aim. If children can simply enjoy listening out for and having a go at identifying the sounds that make up our language, they will have taken a huge step along the path towards reading and writing.

Chapter 3: Matching Sound and Symbol

Chapter 3 focuses on linking the different sounds of language with the symbols that represent those sounds. *Curriculum Guidance for the Foundation Stage* states that children should be able to name and sound the letters of the alphabet by the end of the Reception year; the *National Literacy Strategy* adds the phonemes and graphemes for *ch*, *sh* and *th*, while the DfES guidance *Playing with Sounds* specifies a number of double graphemes and consonant blends such as *ll*, *ss*, *wh* and *ng* (see page 4 for a full list).

The 26 letters of the alphabet make up the basic building blocks of written language – and learning to associate these symbols with their sounds is an essential first step towards reading and writing. However, a fully competent reader will also need to recognize digraphs such as the *Playing with Sounds* double graphemes, other common consonant blends (such as *br*, *cl*), vowel blends (such as *ai*, *oa*), common letter clusters (such as *str*, *igh*) and the many phonetically irregular words in the English language (such as *she*, *who*). Although the activities in this chapter concentrate mostly on the letters of the alphabet, make sure that you also provide a literate setting with lots of books and other forms of print. Much of young children's literacy learning is 'untaught' in the sense that they will constantly be absorbing written language – as long as they have lots of daily, ongoing exposure to a print-rich environment. For a more detailed look at this aspect of literacy development, see Chapter 1, Organizing the setting, see pages 12–18 and Chapter 5, Reading in the Environment, pages 76–8.

This chapter is divided into four sections – **Introducing letters**, **Practising letters**, **Exploring letters** and **The alphabet**.

Introducing letters

Children should have experienced listening out for the initial sound of a word, before being introduced to the corresponding letter for that sound. Introducing letters can follow on as an adjunct to many sound games such as *Playing with alliteration* and *I spy*. In this respect, the activities in this chapter should be regarded as overlapping those of Chapter 2 (**The Sounds of Language**).

The **Textured letters** (pages 38–40) make a useful key resource for introducing letter symbols. Learning to recognize letters is a preparation for letter formation (writing) as well as reading, and the textured shape enables the children to feel how the letter is written. Always check that the child is tracing the letter in the same way as it is written; laying sound foundations at this early stage is invaluable for later handwriting.

Practising letters/Exploring letters

Children need lots of opportunity to reinforce their knowledge of sound/letter links. Most of the activities in the **Practising letters** section require the children to be active, moving around the setting and handling real objects. Many of the activities encourage the children to identify a given letter within a CVC word. As part of the activity, you can also model the process of sounding out/blending sounds to read the whole word – a precursor to **The reading basket** and other activities in Chapter 5 (**Becoming a Reader**).

Apart from day-to-day exposure to letters through books, signs, notices and other environmental print, children should be helped to find familiar letters in words, books and chunks of text. This gives them the all-important opportunity to experience letters within their natural context. The activities in the **Exploring letters** section encourage children to search for letters in magazines, newspapers and books, as well as introducing the many different font styles to be found within the world of print.

The alphabet

The names of the letters (as opposed to the sounds they make) are not of much use when it comes to decoding the printed word. For this reason, letter names and upper case letters should only be introduced once the child has established the link between sounds and lower case letters. If the child has had lots of experience of books and other forms of environmental print, capital letters should already be quite familiar. Learning the order of the alphabet is also not necessary for the basics of reading and writing. However, alphabetical order is used in many different kinds of literature, particularly dictionaries, encyclopaedias and indexes. For this reason, older children should learn to recite the alphabet through pleasurable activities such as songs, games, looking at alphabet books and making alphabet charts.

Chapter 4: Becoming a Writer

Writing is a complex activity that brings together many different strands. In order to become a 'whole' writer, there are three main areas of capability that the child needs to develop:

- ■ **The content:** deciding on what your piece of writing is going to say; choosing the words to fit the purpose of the communication; organizing those words so that they make sense and deciding on an appropriate writing format. For example, a poem generally uses different kinds of words and a different layout compared with a shopping list.

■ **Word building:** the ability to segment a word into its separate sounds and represent those sounds with symbols, as well as the ability to spell irregular words such as *the* or *where*.

■ **Handwriting:** the ability to manipulate a writing implement to represent the words on paper.

Segmenting words into their separate sounds and linking sounds with letters has been covered in Chapters 2 and 3. In this chapter, the focus is on developing a controlled and co-ordinated hand, letter formation, word building and writing simple words, exploring opportunities to write and using different writing formats.

The chapter is divided into three sections – **Pre-writing activities**, **Handwriting** and **Content**.

Pre-writing activities

Lots of preparation is essential to the development of physical writing skills. The ***Developing muscular strength and co-ordination*** activities focus on ways of refining hand/eye co-ordination and developing strength in the three writing digits (the thumb, index and middle fingers).

Discovering that you can change the appearance of a surface is one of the first steps towards seeing oneself as 'a writer'. Through the ***Mark making and patterning*** activities, children can explore the act of mark making, with all its many possibilities. These activities also enable the children to make the kind of hand and arm movements that will later be translated into writing letters and words on paper.

Handwriting

As children gain experience of print through books and other forms of writing, learn their letters and develop the ability to manipulate a writing implement, their mark making takes on a more 'writing-like' quality. The opportunity to freely explore writing materials is an essential part of this process. ***Writing letters with chalk and pencil*** can be introduced if necessary, but it is important not to push a reluctant child. Tracing the ***Textured letters*** with the fingers, ***Writing letters in air*** and ***Writing letters in sand*** are useful precursors to the more permanent act of writing on paper.

Investigating letter formation can also help the development of handwriting. The ***Exploring letter shapes*** activities offer ways of discovering the many different features of lower case letters. Always remember that letters in isolation are ultimately meaningless. As you explore letter shapes and writing letters, keep on providing a context by looking for the letter within words, books, notices and other environmental print.

Content

The activities in this section cover what is perhaps the most important element of writing – its content. As an introduction to writing words, start off with the child's name. Apart from being a familiar *spoken* word, children will already have had lots of opportunity to explore the sounds and letters that make up their name. ***The word basket*** activity goes on to introduce the process of segmenting a CVC word into its separate sounds and representing those sounds with cut-out letters. This process enables the children to 'write' simple words, without the additional challenge of handling a writing implement or coping with letter formation.

Building and writing single words is, however, just one small aspect of becoming a whole writer. To enable children to experience the process of 'writing', use ***Dictation*** techniques to scribe their thoughts, ideas and messages. Always write in front of the children, to help them absorb the purpose and process of writing. The next stage on from ***Dictation*** is ***Shared writing***. This activity encourages children to use their emergent writing skills by helping you, the writer, to construct sentences, build words and organize the writing on the page. Children should also be encouraged to write freely and independently (***Independent writing***). This can range from younger children creating meaningful marks and 'writing-like' representations, to older able children writing extensively.

In order for ***Dictation***, ***Shared writing*** and ***Independent writing*** to take place, you and your children will need something to write about. The ***Opportunities to write*** activities offer many ideas for both content and format. Children learn best when they participate in meaningful activities, and these writing opportunities are all based around real-life situations – composing a letter for home, writing notices for the setting. Part of becoming a whole writer includes being able to choose from a wide range of writing options, in order to fulfil the purpose of your communication. To this end, the ***Opportunities to write*** activities also look at some of the many different formats available to the writer, including lists, captions and letters.

Most important of all, children should be helped to enjoy writing, at whatever stage they have reached. Never push children into formal writing activities before they are ready. Avoid correcting the spelling of those children who are starting to write independently and make sure you provide lots of stimulating writing materials and writing related play opportunities (see Chapter 1, **The Setting**).

Chapter 5: Becoming a Reader

Like writing, reading is a complex activity that brings together lots of different skills. To become a competent reader, the individual needs to develop four areas of capability:

- **Phonics:** the ability to read letters, digraphs, common letter clusters and use phonic knowledge to tackle unfamiliar words.

- **Sight recognition:** the ability to recognize common irregular words, gradually reaching the stage where all words are read by sight.

- **Reading clues:** the ability to use various strategies to make sense of the text. For example, knowledge of common sentence structure, drawing on picture cues and overall context.

- **Reading experience:** familiarity with the many different forms of written language – stories, information books, notices, captions, lists and so on.

In conjunction with the writing activities from Chapter 4, the activities in this chapter provide a foundation for each of these areas. The chapter is divided into three sections – **Reading in the environment**, **Reading activities: words** and **Reading activities: phrases and sentences**.

Reading in the environment

Reading in the environment begins from day one in that children are constantly exposed to signs, notices and other environmental print. The activities in this section encourage children to start reading within their surroundings. ***Reading notices and signs*** gets the children looking out for everyday print to be found in the setting and beyond, while **A *wrappings chart*** explores the print on familiar food containers.

Reading activities: words

Children approach the printed word in various ways when they first start to read. ***The reading basket*** introduces the phonic technique of identifying and blending sounds in order to read simple CVC words. It makes a good starting point for reading and gives the children some useful word attack techniques to draw on later in their reading careers (try giving an unfamiliar word to Key Stage 2 children with poor phonics knowledge, and you soon discover that that they don't know where to begin!).

Phonics is, however, just a small part of the reading story. Many words in the English language have to be sight learnt, and some children respond better to word recognition than a phonic approach. The ***High frequency word activities*** offer lots of ways to sight learn the words from *The National Literacy Strategy* list for Reception. Each activity explores the words within the context of a meaningful chunk of text. This is particularly important here. Unlike an object name or action word, it is difficult to get across the meaning of words such as *all* or *she* out of context.

Practice and reinforcement are essential to reading development. The ***Word games*** encourage children to use their developing reading skills by approaching new words. Each game starts off with simple CVC words, moving on to more complex words as the children grow in confidence. As always with reading, meaning is important, and the games encourage the children to act on the word they have just read. For example, performing an action word in ***The 'I can' game*** or using a word card as a label for different items in ***Labelling the setting***.

Once children can cope with simple CVC words, they need to discover that the same words will appear in different contexts. **A *reading flap book*** enables children to revisit familiar words, while ***Rime sorting boxes*** help children to explore groups of CVC words with a similar spelling pattern.

Reading activities: phrases and sentences

The ***Phrase and sentence games*** introduce the next step: tackling words within the context of a sentence. As with the ***Word games***, the children are required to act upon what they have just read – and in order to interpret the meaning of the sentence or phrase, they have to read it in its entirety. For example, you need all the words in the phrase '*put the teddy under the chair*' to know *how* and *where* to position the teddy.

Once children have started to approach texts in a 'readerly' manner, they can be encouraged to help you read a text during a ***Shared reading*** session. Shared reading is a useful means of introducing and reinforcing various reading strategies as well as exploring the meaning of the text.

Chapter 6: The Role of the Picture Book

The picture book is perhaps the single most important resource when it comes to literacy development. Through exploring picture books, the children will make all kinds of discoveries about literacy and the reading process. For example:

- The many different purposes of books – information, pleasure, reference.

- The appearance of print on the page and the opportunity to absorb printed letters, common letter clusters and words.

- The chance to witness the process of reading – how the reader looks at the printed page and translates it into meaningful spoken language.

- Learning how a story 'works'.

- Becoming familiar and comfortable with books, embracing them as a natural part of everyday life.

The chapter is divided into three sections – **Sharing picture books, Exploring picture books** and **Story structure**.

Sharing picture books

The process of sharing picture books is, in many ways, similar to ***Shared reading*** (Chapter 5). However, whereas ***Shared reading*** encourages the children to use their developing reading strategies, the ***Sharing picture books*** activities focus on the pleasures of the story.

Most of the learning opportunities offered by a picture book will be greatly enhanced if you can share it on a one-to-one or small group basis. In an individual picture book sharing session, children can see the printed page as you read and you can stop and converse about whatever interests them. Using books independently is also essential to the child's early reading experience (***Using books independently***). Ultimately, reading is a private activity. When children start to look at books by themselves, they are taking a huge step forward in identifying themselves as 'readers'.

Exploring picture books

Authors, illustrators and publishers are endlessly creative as to what a modern picture book can embrace. This results in a huge range of possibilities for children to explore – from 'smelly' books and intricate moving parts to a wide selection of themes, topics and subject matter. The ***Different types of books*** activities help the children to discover just how much the world of books has to offer. They also help the child to categorize and make sense of what can seem an overwhelming number of choices.

The book is a physical object as well as the purveyor of abstract information, and children need to discover and identify its many different parts. One of the best ways of helping children to find their way around a book is to get them designing, constructing, writing and illustrating their own. Along with ***The author and illustrator*** activities, making books also enables the children to explore the idea that real people wrote and illustrated the books in their book corner.

Story structure

Knowing how a story works is fundamental to becoming fully literate. As a starting point, the ***Character*** activities show children who the story is 'about'. Once they know who to focus on, they can engage with that character and follow its fortunes throughout the book.

'The setting' is another important aspect of understanding a story. The ***Story settings*** activities focus on where the events of a story take place, linking the concept to the children's own experiences by encouraging them to explore the settings within their own lives.

The third narrative element in this section is 'the plot': what actually happens in the story. The ***Plot*** activities encourage the children to focus on narrative elements such as the sequence of events, cause and effect and endings. This focus is important in helping children to become committed readers; after all, it is wanting to find out what happens next that keeps you going right up to the end.

Last but very definitely not least, children should be encouraged to retell familiar stories in their own words (***Recounting stories***). This gives them the opportunity to use their knowledge of character, setting and plot through reconstructing the events of a familiar book or making up their own stories.

The Setting

In this chapter ...

The playful exploration of books, story props and writing materials is central to the young child's literacy development. In order to encourage such exploration, the early years practitioner needs to focus on:

■ creating a print-rich and literate play environment

■ working with groups within setting.

The first part of this chapter looks at the provision of resources and play opportunities linked to the sounds of language, exploring letters, reading and writing within the environment and picture books.

The second part of the chapter looks at working with groups and includes some thoughts on group size and make up, timing, location, a positive approach, using assistants and encouraging impromptu and child-led group activities.

Organizing the setting

The sounds of language

To help children explore the sounds of language, put out lots of activities linked to nursery rhymes and sound games.

Nursery rhyme corner: set up a separate nursery rhyme area or devote a corner of the book area to traditional rhymes. Include some or all of the following:

■ A selection of nursery rhyme books, displayed on a low table along with some floor cushions. Make sure that the collection represents a range of different cultures and traditions.

- A cassette player with headphones and tapes of nursery rhymes. Pre-set the volume so that children can't turn it up too loud.

- Nursery rhyme cards: choose a selection of key rhymes to represent the different elements that you will be exploring in relation to the sounds of language. For example, *Lavender's Blue* (**Clapping rhymes**, page 21, *Baa, Baa, Black Sheep* (**Playing with alliteration**, pages 26–9). Include rhymes to reflect different cultures and traditions. Write out, illustrate and laminate the rhymes so that they can be stored in the nursery rhyme corner.

- Wall space for displaying children's work and nursery rhyme posters.

- Dressing up clothes and props linked to one or two nursery rhymes.

- Nursery rhyme packs: these can be stored in the nursery rhyme corner for children to explore independently, and also be sent home. Include the following:

  ✓ Nursery rhyme card.

  ✓ Small nursery rhyme book.

  ✓ Tape with different versions of the rhyme – for example, an adult reciting the rhyme, a piano accompaniment, children singing the rhyme, beating out the rhythm with percussion instruments.

  ✓ Small play props – for example, the *Jack and Jill* pack might contain a toy pail, two dolls to represent Jack and Jill, some real brown paper and a bottle marked 'vinegar'.

  ✓ Activity sheets/coloured pencils – for example, asking the child to draw different parts of the rhyme (keep the master copy to replace photocopies as they get used up).

  ✓ For emergent readers, packs of word cards and activities linked to the rhyme – for example, groups of rhyming words to sort.

  ✓ Set of instructions, explaining how home carers can help children get the most from the pack.

Sound activities: some of the sound detection games can be displayed in the setting for children to explore independently:

- Put out objects from **The rhyme basket** (pages 24–6). Encourage the children to play with the objects and put them in their rhyme groups.

- Put out the objects from **Digging up sounds** (pages 31–2) in an old wooden casket, alongside a box of pirate dressing up clothes. Encourage the children to name and identify the initial sounds of the 'treasure' as they play at being pirates.

- Put out the puppet from **End sound puppet** (page 36), along with a box of appropriate items, and encourage children to role play being 'teacher' and 'pupil'.

Change the items in the displays from time to time, to spark new interest in the activity.

Exploring letters

Setting up letter displays is invaluable in helping young children to absorb the letter shapes. Provide some or all of the following:

Alphabet books and friezes: display a wide selection of alphabet books in the book corner and put up alphabet friezes in the writing area and elsewhere in the setting. Choose friezes with both lower case and upper case letters. Check that the pictures include the names of the objects, preferably with the initial letter underlined.

Letter resources: display letter cards such as the **_Textured letters_** (see pages 38–40) along a shelf so that the children can see them constantly. Provide magnetic, foam, plastic and wooden letters for children to explore. Set up a **_Letter washing line_** (page 41) for displaying letters and ensure that your letter flags and puppets are available for children to play with. Use fabric paint to decorate t-shirts, hats and aprons with individual letters and put them in the dressing up box.

Letter games and puzzles: make **_Letter lotto_** (pages 46–7) and other letter games available for children to play with independently. Purchase some good quality wooden letter puzzles, including capital letter puzzles for older children (see **Useful resources**, page 54).

Becoming a writer/Becoming a reader

Because of the link between reading and writing, many literacy related resources and play areas will support and develop both skills. As you plan for literacy development in your setting, include the following:

The writing area: aim to offer a wide range of different materials and writing opportunities in the writing area. At the same time, make sure you don't swamp the children with too much choice. Build up a selection of materials little by little, introducing just one or two items at a time. Every week or so, set out a new activity linked to a particular topic or story:

- Following a cooking session, put out blank recipe cards with different coloured pens or pencils (see **Photocopiable Writing Framework 2 / recipe**).

- During the lead up to Diwali or Christmas, put out folded blank cards with silver and gold pens, sticky stars and other materials, so that children can make and write their own greetings cards (check that the pens are safe for independent use).

- After making a group book (see **_Making books_**, pages 96–8) or exploring a particular story, put out copies of the book along with some blank books. Encourage the children to write and illustrate their own books, either a version of the story or something new.

The following list covers some of the main resources that you can include in your writing area:

- Writing tables and chairs, positioned in good, natural light.

- Computer.

- Large, free standing blackboards and whiteboards with different coloured chalk/marker pens and erasers.

- Small blackboards/whiteboards, some with lines.

- Clipboards with a pencil attached to a string.

- A name card holder (page 62), word bank and ***High frequency word bank*** (page 80) plus strips of paper so that children can write their own names and words.

- Cut-out letters for independent exploration and word building (wooden, foam, magnetic, plastic).

- Wall space for displaying children's work and other handwritten and printed literature.

- A range of different papers, including:
  - ✓ assorted shapes, sizes and colours
  - ✓ lined/unlined
  - ✓ blank notebooks
  - ✓ post-it notes/sticky labels
  - ✓ writing paper, envelopes and used stamps
  - ✓ photocopied 'writing frameworks' such as blank lists and speech bubbles (see **Photocopiable Writing Frameworks**, pages 73–5)
  - ✓ old forms and leaflets.

- A range of writing and mark-making implements:
  - ✓ pencils, regular size and chunky, including a range of grades from H to 2B
  - ✓ coloured pencils, including metallic, rainbow stripes, skin tones
  - ✓ non-toxic felt pens
  - ✓ wax crayons
  - ✓ coloured chalk/charcoal.

- Other writing accessories, including:
  - ✓ scissors
  - ✓ rubbers

✓ paper clips and other paper fasteners

✓ Sellotape, parcel tape and other kinds of tape

✓ hole puncher

✓ stampers and printing sets.

Notice boards and post boxes: notice boards and post boxes are great for getting children to read and write, as well as helping them to discover the purpose of messages, notes and letters. Construct your own notice board by pinning a trellis of sturdy fabric tape to a board so messages can be tucked behind the tape. You can also provide a letter-box to be emptied by a designated postperson. Use the notice board and post box to send notes to each child. Link the notes to favourite stories, activities, topics and significant events in the child's life. Match the notes to the reading level of each child so that they can read them as independently as possible. Younger ones can be sent a special picture with their name on.

Role-play settings: include lots of role-play reading and writing opportunities. For example, set up a telephone, telephone directory, message pad and pencil in the home corner; display advertisement posters and provide blank shopping lists and old receipts in the play shop; turn the book corner into a play library with forms to fill in, library tickets and lots of books to choose from.

Throughout the setting: display notices, captions and other printed material relating to the child's daily experiences. The following are just some of the many reading and writing opportunities you can create within your physical environment:

■ Label boxes, shelves and other storage containers with the name and photo of the item that lives there.

■ Put out written instructions to help the smooth running of the group – *please do not feed the fish/put your boots here.*

■ Label pictures, displays and activities with captions and instructions – *We went to the park on Friday/Can you dig up the treasure?*

■ Set up writing activities throughout the setting. For example, position a large whiteboard or paper flip chart and marker pens next to the window, with the written question: *What is the weather today?* Introduce the activity at the start of the session and encourage the children to respond in their own time with writing and drawing. At the end of the session, read through the different responses with the group. Other similar writing activities could include:

✓ A whiteboard/flip chart in the book corner for children to list the books they have looked at along with their written/drawn responses.

✓ A whiteboard/flipchart by the fish tank or guinea pig hutch for recording who has fed the pets and writing/drawing observations.

Outside: reading and writing related activities should continue outdoors. Provide chunky playground chalk and designated 'graffiti' areas, including blackboards and large sheets of paper taped to a wall. Make marks with water and decorating brushes on a hard outdoor surface. Encourage children to take a clipboard and paper into the garden so they can continue reading and writing outside. Write signs and notices for garden equipment. Set up outdoor whiteboards and encourage the children to record wildlife, the weather and outdoor activities.

Picture books

Books should be integral to every area of the early years setting. There are two main aspects to consider:

■ the book corner

■ displaying books throughout the setting.

The book corner: the book corner should be central to the child's experience of books. Make it welcoming, stimulating and accessible with some or all of the following features:

■ Book shelves, book boxes and book stands. Wherever possible, display the books front outwards. Check that the books are easy to reach.

■ A small number of key books that the group can get to know well.

■ A wide selection of books offering positive messages about racial and cultural diversity, different family types, gender, disability and social/emotional issues such as friendship, kindness and sharing.

■ Colour coding for different categories. For example, label the shelf and each book in the poetry section with a blue label and the letter P.

■ A display table for special collections of books (see ***Different types of books***, pages 94–6).

■ Wall space for posters, children's work and book related displays.

■ Comfortable chairs, floor cushions, bean bags and an attractive floor rug.

■ Space to store book related dressing up clothes and story boards (see ***Recounting stories*** pages 103–4).

■ Picture book packs to be used in the setting and sent home. For example, a pack for Eric Carle's *The Very Hungry Caterpillar* (Puffin) might include:

    ✓ toy caterpillar

    ✓ plastic fruits representing those in the story

    ✓ word cards with the names of the week

✓ coloured crayons/photocopiable activity sheet asking the child to draw the different stages in the caterpillar's life cycle

✓ tape of the story (record your own)

✓ information sheet for parents.

Throughout the setting: books should not just be confined to the book corner. Set up small collections of books beside different activities: a box of books with a vehicle theme near the toy garage; books about fish near the fish tank. Always add related books to any topic display. Provide a box of outdoor books with nature, garden and outdoor play themes. Cover them with sticky-backed plastic and, wherever possible, choose books with wipeable pages.

Working with groups

There are a number of factors to consider when working with groups in the early years setting. As you plan your language and literacy group activities, bear in mind the following:

The size of the group: group size will vary, depending on the nature of the activity and the overall number of children in your setting. As a general rule, keep the group as small as possible when introducing new and complex concepts and processes. Once children are engaged in practising a skill, you can plan for a larger group. If an activity involves turn taking, a small group allows each child to have more turns and so gain greater experience of whatever the activity is offering. Some activities lend themselves to large groups, for example story time or an extended and carefully organized role-play activity. Apart from drawing on your own group management skills, ask assistants to help with such groups, particularly if they include younger children.

The make up of the group: when planning who to include in the group, choose those children who are ready for whatever the activity has to offer. If your setting has a mixed age group, it can also be useful to include an older child in some group activities. Give the older child the first turn, to help show the rest of the group what to do. Aim also to include a mixture of confident and reticent children. Part of functioning within a group includes the ability to operate alongside many different personalities.

A positive approach: think through positive ways of responding to the children and handling different personalities within the group. Help talkative children to draw to a close, without making them feel sidelined. One approach is to remind children that it is someone else's turn, while also explaining that they can continue their conversation with you once the group activity is over. Also consider ways of gently encouraging reticent children to engage with the activity. Persist in inviting them to have a turn, but respond neutrally if they choose not to join in; remember that for some children, simply sitting in a group is a big achievement. Another potentially sensitive area is your response to 'errors'. Avoid flagging up mistakes and, wherever possible, use them as learning opportunities (for a specific example, see the *I spy* **Tips** section, pages 29–31).

Assistants: asking assistants to join in an activity can be very useful for modelling a skill or process. Assistants can also be asked to sit with and support individual children, and help to organize a large group activity such as an extended role play.

Timetabling: the best times to hold a particular group activity will depend on a number of factors, including your physical surroundings and the overall personality of your group. If your children are calm after outdoor play, use this time for focused activities such as linking letters and sounds. If they take a while to settle down, plan for something more active such as clapping rhythms. If you had intended to do some quiet, focused activities and the day turns out to be windy, you may want to rethink your timetable altogether! Have a rough plan of how long you expect an activity to last, but do always allow for extra time. If children have taken off on an activity, you do *not* want to be cutting them off in full flow because it's lunch time. Similarly, if a group is not going well, be prepared to finish it off and rethink your approach, timing or whether the children are ready for the activity.

Location: where you decide to hold your group can make a big difference to how well it goes. Try to choose a quiet area for activities that involve concentration – it's difficult to listen out for the sounds of language when a lively painting session is going on next door! Large group activities can be easier to conduct if you make a circle of chairs – and for this you will need a clear space. Story and nursery rhyme sessions lend themselves well to a more informal arrangement, with the group squashed cosily into the book corner. With any group activity, check that all the children can see and hear what is going on.

Impromptu groups: most important of all, be ready to join in with impromptu groups. Perhaps something has occurred that can be developed into a literacy orientated activity – making a new sign for the setting or exploring a new book. Perhaps a small group of children are busily conducting their own *I spy* or guessing game. Observe, nurture and value such moments – and remember that a child-led, impromptu group activity will always offer the best learning experience of all.

The Sounds of Language

In this chapter ...

This chapter focuses on the sounds that make up spoken language. It is divided into three sections:

- Rhythm and rhyme

- Initial sounds

- Segmenting words.

Rhythm and rhyme

Learning to detect rhyming words and the rhythm of spoken language is the first step in the development of phonological awareness.

Playing with rhythm

The following activities introduce children to the rhythms of language through clapping out the beats of names, nursery rhymes and familiar multisyllabic words. As always, start with the most familiar – the names of the children in the group.

Clapping names

Start off by clapping names with one syllable (*Sam*, *Jim*), then move on to two syllables (*Ma-lik*, *Ras-na*) and three and four syllables (*Rose-ma-ry*, *E-liz-a-beth*). Repeat a single name to create a rhythm:

> *Ma-lik* / *Ma-lik* / *Ma-lik* / *Ma-lik*

Count the number of claps for each name and put two names together to create a repeating rhythm:

Ma-lik-Rose-ma-ry / Ma-lik-Rose-ma-ry
Tom-Ras-na / Tom-Ras-na

⭐ **TIPS**

Clapping names can be useful for new children and those who find it difficult to integrate socially.

Clapping rhymes

Choose a key selection of traditional rhymes (for more information on key rhymes, see Chapter 1, **The Setting**, page 13). Go for rhymes with some multisyllabic words, such as *Lavender's Blue* or *Hickory Dickory Dock*. Help the children to learn the rhymes by singing them as often as possible. As the children become familiar with the rhymes, start to clap their rhythm. Emphasize segmenting the words into their separate syllables – *lav-en-der*, *hick-o-ry*, *in-cy win-cy*.

⭐ **TIPS**

Explore rhymes from a range of cultural traditions. If possible, invite visitors from different cultural backgrounds to share some of their own childhood rhymes.

Clapping words

Make outline drawings of different creatures on A5 cards. Keep the drawings simple as they need to be immediately recognizable. Choose one creature with a single syllable name (*pig*, *dog*, *ant*), one with a two syllable name (*pup-py*, *kit-ty*, *pan-da*) and one with a three syllable name (*bum-ble-bee*, *el-e-phant*, *kang-a-roo*). Name the animals and practise clapping out the syllables as you say their names. When the children can do this easily, hold up a card as the trigger for saying/clapping the rhythm of the name. Gradually introduce holding up a card as a trigger for clapping the rhythm without saying the word. Try interspersing cards to build rhythm patterns such as:

pup-py-bum-ble-bee / pup-py-bum-ble-bee

⭐ **TIPS**

Practise holding up and putting down one card with the left hand and one with the right in a back and forth sequence, to create a smooth rhythm.

✓ **READINESS**

Start singing traditional rhymes and clapping out the rhythms of the children's names as soon as they arrive in your setting. Repeat these activities over and over again so that the children become familiar with the rhymes and adept at picking up rhythms.

Playing with rhyme

Playing with rhyming words is a great way to develop phonological awareness – and older children can be surprisingly creative when it comes to making up their own rhymes.

Traditional rhymes

Once children know a traditional rhyme well, miss out the rhyming words for them to fill in:

> *Hickory, Dickory …*
> *The mouse ran up the …*

Choose rhymes with monosyllabic rhyming words such as *Jack and **Jill*** and slip in some new rhyming words:

> *Hickory Dickory Dock*
> *The mouse ran up the **sock** (or rock/lock/clock)*

Try slipping in some non-rhyming words:

> *Humpty Dumpty sat on the **wall***
> *Humpty Dumpty had a big **bump***

⭐ TIPS

Use facial and vocal expression to alert the children to a non-rhyming or nonsense word, and wait for them to pounce on your 'mistake'.

The rhymes do not have to make sense – in fact, the children will enjoy nonsense elements such as the mouse running up a sock.

Encourage older/able children to explore made up words – the mouse could run up the '*bock*' or Jack and Jill could go up the '*shill*'. Can they come up with meanings for their new words?

Introduce a different form of communication by creating signs for a particular rhyme. For example, make an egg shape with the arms to represent *Humpty Dumpty*.

Made up rhymes

Make up your own rhymes for the children to finish. Start off by supplying the rhyming words yourself and gradually ease the children into thinking up words for themselves. Encourage them to come up with lots of rhyming words, to create a rhyming string. The following are just a few examples of verses that can be adapted to offer different rhyming possibilities:

> *FRED THE CAT*
> *Down behind the bushes*
> *I met a cat called Fred*
> *He says he's very hungry*
> *And he's going to eat a … (bed / bread / shed / head / ted)*

Explore different rhyming words by changing the cat's name – *Bill* (*hill/pill*); *Ben* (*hen/pen*); *Ann* (*can/fan*); *Matt* (*hat/cat*).

> *THE WINDOW*
> *Look through the window*
> *What can you see?*
> *I can see a big dog*
> *Sitting on a … (bee/tree/pea/sea/flea/me)*

Explore different rhyming words by changing *see* in line 2 to *spot* (*cot/dot*) or *spy* (*fly/pie*).

★ TIPS

You do not have to come up with a whole verse – a couple of lines will do, such as: '*My name is Ben / I'm sitting on a …*'.

Encourage older/able children to think about how wording should be changed to fit their chosen rhyme. For example, *sitting on me* sounds better than *sitting on a me* (see *The Window*, above).

This is my chin

Make up a list of familiar words that rhyme with parts of the body, such as:

> *chin/bin head/bed hair/chair eye/tie knee/tea*
> *ear/beer leg/peg hand/band nail/tail face/lace*

Choose a part of the body, such as the head, point to it and sing: '*this is my head*'. Use any familiar tune, such as the first few notes of a nursery rhyme. Show the children how to sing in reply: '*yes, it's your head*'. When the children are familiar with the routine, slip in a 'mistake' by using a word that rhymes with the body part. For example, point to the chin and sing: '*this is my bin*'. Discuss the mistake, emphasizing that the word *bin* rhymes with the body part *chin*. Demonstrate that the children now need to sing: '*no, it's your chin*'.

23

⭐ **TIPS**

Link this activity to a topic on 'Ourselves' or 'Our Bodies'.

Use facial and vocal expression to alert the children to your deliberate 'mistake'.

Be clear about which part of the body you are pointing to so that the children can tell the difference between 'face' and 'head' or 'nail' and 'finger'.

✓ **READINESS**

Start introducing traditional rhymes as soon as the children arrive in the setting. In order to spot a rhyming error, children need to be able to discriminate between rhyming and non-rhyming words. Ideally, children should know a rhyme well before playing around with it.

CURRICULUM GUIDANCE

Yellow stepping stone: *enjoy rhyming and rhythmic activities*
Blue stepping stone: *show awareness of rhyme ...*
Green stepping stone: *continue a rhyming string*
NLS/WORD: *recognising, exploring and working with rhyming patterns* (DfEE, 1998)

The rhyme basket

Young children love any activity that involves real objects to handle and explore.

Resources

✓ A basket containing a collection of objects or pictures with rhyming names:

Pairs

cat/hat pen/ten ship/zip dog/log mug/bug dot/cot
sun/bun chain/train bee/key boat/coat meat/feet

Groups

cat / hat / bat / rat / mat
shed / bed / red / ted / head
clock / rock / sock / lock / block
chair / bear / hair / pear / square

For numbers, use a card with the symbol (e.g. '10'). Include photos of any children whose names fit into a rhyming group, for example, *Sam, Matt*. Once you have made up your Rhyme basket, store it for later use. Keep a stock of appropriate items to draw from so that you can keep on offering new rhyming experiences.

Pairing activity

Gather together pairs of objects with rhyming names. Talk about and name the objects and let the children handle them. If necessary, finish the activity at this stage and carry on the next day.

- Start off with just two or three pairs. Choose objects with clearly contrasting onsets and rimes, for example *sock* / *rock* and *bat* / *hat* rather than *Ben* / *pen* and *bin* / *pin*.

- Set out one object from each pair on a mat and place the remaining objects in a basket.

- Ask a child to pick an object from the basket and name it.

- Go through the names of the objects on the mat.

- Ask the children to decide which 'mat' object has a rhyming name and place the 'basket' object alongside.

- When all the objects have been paired, go through the names, isolating the onset from the rime to show how the words rhyme – *h-at*, *c-at* / *s-ock*, *r-ock*.

- Gradually build up to matching several pairs of objects as the children get to grips with the game.

Sorting activity

Gather together groups of objects with rhyming names. Introduce them in the same way as the pairing activity.

- Start off with just two groups of three objects.

- Place one object from each of the two groups on a floor mat, to act as a 'marker' for the group, and put the remaining objects in the basket.

- Ask a child to pick an object from the basket, name it and decide which of the two marker objects its name rhymes with.

- When all the objects have been sorted, go through the names in each rhyme group, isolating the onset from the rime – *p-en*, *m-en*, *h-en*.

- Slowly build up to several rhyme groups, each containing a number of objects.

★ TIPS

The use of an interesting object can help children to engage in the game, although do make sure that it does not distract them from the purpose of the activity.

✓ **READINESS**

Introduce this game once children have had experience of rhyming words through nursery rhymes and rhyming texts. Give plenty of support to begin with and then gradually withdraw so that the children are doing the activity independently.

CURRICULUM GUIDANCE

Yellow stepping stone: *enjoy rhyming activities*

Blue stepping stone: *show awareness of rhyme ...*

Green stepping stone: *continue a rhyming string*

NLS/WORD: *recognising, exploring and working with rhyming patterns*

Initial sounds

The activities in this section focus on the initial sounds of words. This is the first step in the process of detecting the individual phonemes that make up a word.

Playing with alliteration

Alliteration is a useful language tool for encouraging children to focus on a particular initial sound.

Alliterative nursery rhymes

Choose some alliterative nursery rhymes such as *Baa, Baa, Black Sheep* or *Lucy Locket*. Once the children are familiar with the rhymes, pick out the repeated initial sound. Can the children think of other words beginning with the same sound? Try fitting them into the rhyme. For example, *Georgie Porgie, pepper and pie*.

Have you any wellies?

Sing '*Baa, baa, black sheep/Have you any wool?*' but instead of *wool*, insert the name of another item beginning with *w* – '*Baa, baa, black sheep/Have you any wellies/water/wigs?*' Choose different items and come up with strings of words beginning with the same sound – '*Have you any sausages, sandals, snakes?*'

Once the children have had some experience of a particular sound, you can introduce its corresponding letter (see **Textured letters**, pages 38–40).

⭐ **TIPS**

Add to the fun by asking children to pick items from a bag. Use the item as the first word and then follow on with other items beginning with the same sound. For example, if the child picks out a book, you could go on to list *bag, biscuits* and *bottles*.

Role-play sounds

Show the children how to repeat a particular phoneme to create sound effects for short role-play scenarios. Try the following:

- *sh-sh-sh-sh* – settling a baby
- *ch-ch-ch-ch* – train driver
- *h-h-h-h* (voiceless expiration of breath) – blowing out a candle
- *d-d-d-d* – builder using hammer or drill
- *rrrr-rrrr-rrrr* – growling dog
- *u-u-u-u* – tugging on a rope
- *zzzz-zzzz-zzzz* – buzzy bees
- *mmm-mmm-mmm* – wailing babies
- *a-a-a-a* – telling someone off
- *ssss-ssss-ssss* – hissing snake
- *ee-ee-ee-ee* – squeaking mouse.

Once the children have had some experience of a particular sound, you can introduce its corresponding letter (see ***Textured letters***, paes 38–40).

⭐ TIPS

Ask an assistant to help model the role play, if necessary.

Introduce props, for example a whistle and peaked cap for the *ch-ch-ch-ch* role play. Encourage the children to develop the role plays in their own way.

Finger folk sounds

Select up to six different sounds and draw six faces on small card circles. Ask the children to help you choose alliterative names for the characters. Take the children's first names as a starting point, for example *Cally Careful, Billy Bounce, Sunny Sanjit*. As an alternative to people, make animal heads and choose names such as *Eddy Elephant*. Decide as a group which names you like best for a particular face. Using double sided sticky tape, attach the faces to the thumb, index and middle fingertips of each hand. Hide your hands behind your back while you sing the first two lines – '*Charlie Cheerful, Charlie Cheerful, where are you?*' (to the tune of *Peter Pointer*). Hold up one finger with the appropriate face while you sing the rest of the song – '*here's Charlie Cheerful, here's Charlie Cheerful, how do you do?*'

Once the children have had some experience of a particular sound, you can introduce its corresponding letter (see ***Textured letters***, pages 38–40).

⭐ TIPS

Develop characters to fit into a particular topic. For example, 'Pets': *Polly Puppy*, *Harry Hamster*; 'People Who Help Us': *Betty Bus Driver*, *Nurse Nick*.

Give the children puppets or soft toys so that they can join in with the actions.

Prepare in advance a list of appropriate adjectives for each child in the group. If you can't think of a suitable adjective (such as *Charlie **Cheerful***) go for an appealing noun (such as *Alex **Apple***).

It can be useful to make a written note of which face is on which finger, before embarking on the song. For example – *Charlie Cheerful, left index*.

Action tongue twisters

Make up a selection of action tongue twisters, such as:

> *bounce the ball*
> *chew the cheese*
> *jump over the jumper*
> *hop happily over the hat*
> *wobble William*
> *pat Peter*
> *stroke Stefan softly*
> *ruffle Rashid*
> *cuddle Katie*
> *tap Tanita*

Identify the alliterative sound in the tongue twister and then ask the children to perform the action, using props where necessary. Repeat the phrase and go through the alliterative sounds again, before moving on to a new tongue twister. Encourage older ones to make up their own action tongue twisters.

Once the children have had some experience of a particular sound, you can introduce its letter (see ***Textured letters***, pages 38–40).

⭐ TIPS

Check that William and Rashid do not mind being wobbled and ruffled!

Prepare in advance a list of action words that alliterate with the names of all the children in the group. If you can't come up with an action word, choose a role: for example, *Eddie engine driver* (ask Eddie to role play driving an engine).

The physical nature of this activity can be useful for children who find it difficult to sit still. Be ready to help a child end the action at the appropriate moment.

The 'action' element of the activity enables you to check that the meaning of the phrase has been understood and acted upon. This can be useful for children who have difficulty in following instructions.

✓ READINESS

Children of all ages can join in these activities. As children become ready, encourage them to identify the alliterative sound and make up their own alliterative phrases.

CURRICULUM GUIDANCE

Yellow stepping stone: *distinguish one sound from another*

Blue stepping stone: *show awareness of ... alliteration*

Green stepping stone: *hear and say the initial sound in words ...*

NLS/WORD: *hearing and identifying initial sounds in words; identifying alliteration in known ... words*

I spy with my little eye

Playing *I spy* helps children to listen out for and detect the phonemes of spoken language. Unlike traditional *I spy*, the focus here is on the sounds of language. This means that we ask for something beginning with the sound made by a letter (*a* as in *apple*), rather than the name of a letter (*Ay*). Spelling is also not a concern at this stage; *kite* and *cat* would both be correct answers for '*I spy something beginning with the sound c*', while *Charlotte* would be a correct answer for '*I spy someone whose name begins with sh*'.

The game can be played as a planned group activity with selected objects, or as a quick 'one-off' with just a couple of children. Slip in a couple of *I spy* turns throughout the day – in the cloakroom, the garden or during lunch.

Resources

✓ A collection of familiar objects whose names begin with the initial sounds that you wish to introduce.

Choose items that appeal to the children, such as a toy *astronaut* for *a* and a cuddly *cat* for *c*. Include items for the three common consonant blends – *sh*, *ch* and *th*. Save the objects to use again and build up a stock so that you can ring the changes.

The *I spy* steps

As a preparation for *I spy*, the children need to be able to identify many of the objects in their immediate environment. Start off by naming objects in the setting, including the parts of the body and items of clothing. Do this as often as possible and slip in little 'naming objects' activities at odd moments throughout the day.

Step 1

- Choose two or three familiar objects, such as a pencil, a cup and a sock, and allow the children to handle and explore them.

- Pick up one of the objects, such as the pencil, look at it and then say – '*I spy with my little eye something beginning with p*'.

- Ask a child to name the object you are holding.

- Reiterate that *pencil* begins with the sound *p* and ask the children to repeat the sound.

- Continue with different objects for as long as the group is interested.

- Once the children have had some experience of a particular sound, you can introduce its corresponding letter (see ***Textured letters***, pages 38–40, and ***I spy with letters***, page 42).

- When the children have had lots of experience and are able to repeat the sounds successfully, move on to Step 2.

★ TIPS

Keep reiterating the correct pronunciation of sounds in a positive and supportive way. For example, a child might mispronounce the initial sound of *goat* as '*d*'. You can reply: '*yes, Sarah, goat begins with the sound* g' and ask the children to repeat the sound a few times.

Step 2

- Choose about six familiar objects with contrasting initial sounds. For example, *pencil*, *cup*, *sock*, *chair*, *leaf* and *apple*. At this stage, avoid objects with similar sounding initial letters, such as *b* and *p* or *a* and *e*. Try to use items that the children are familiar with from Step 1.

- Name and explore the objects, if necessary.

- Put two objects on the table, such as the *pencil* and the *sock*, and say: '*I spy with my little eye something beginning with s*'.

- Challenge the children to give you the object beginning with *s*.

- Continue with different objects, gradually building up the number of choices as the children become more able to detect the initial sound of an object.

Step 3

Once the children can identify initial sounds with confidence, move on to playing a more traditional version of *I spy*:

- Pick a part of the setting such as the writing area and make sure there are plenty of objects beginning with the chosen sound (if necessary, plant objects – for example, put out a *cup*, a *calendar*, a *kite* and a *cushion*).

- Say to the children '*I spy with my little eye something beginning with c in the writing area*' and proceed with the game.

- Gradually progress to spying something within the whole room or garden.

- Encourage the children to lead the group and play the game independently.

⭐ TIPS

Link *I spy* to a particular topic by choosing related items. For example, if you are looking at 'Transport', you could use a toy bus, car, plane and train.

Children's names are always a good starting point for exploring sounds. Try '*I spy with my little eye someone whose name begins with …*'

Parts of the body are useful for quick, one-off games – '*I spy with my little eye a part of my body beginning with …*'. Link with a topic on 'Ourselves' or 'Our Bodies'.

✓ READINESS

Begin naming items as soon as children arrive in the setting. Introduce Step 1 of *I spy* after some experience of rhyming words and clapping activities. Move on to the next step as children become ready. Always follow the pace of the child. With a mixed ability/age group, adapt each question to the child, using Step 1 with one child, Step 3 with the next and so on.

CURRICULUM GUIDANCE

Yellow stepping stone: *distinguish one sound from another*

Green stepping stone: *hear and say the initial sound in words …*

NLS / WORD: *hearing and identifying initial sounds in words*

More initial sound games

Children need lots of opportunity to explore the sounds of language. The following activities aim to reinforce the process of detecting initial sounds.

Digging up sounds

Make a collection of treasure such as *necklaces, beads, pennies, sequins, crystals, shells* and *keys*. Bury the items in the sand box and ask a small group of children to dig up the treasure. Name the items with younger ones and identify the initial sound. Encourage older ones to identify the initial sound for themselves. You can also introduce the corresponding letters for some of the sounds (see **Textured letters**, pages 38–40, and **Digging up letters**, page 42).

★ TIPS

Explore the topic of 'Pirates' with older children. Dress up as pirates and role play 'sailing' off to search for the hidden treasure.

Hunt the sound

Gather together groups of familiar objects that share the same initial sound. For example:

> *pot, pencil, paintbrush, picture, panda*
> *cat, cup, comb, carrot, candle*
> *television, teddy, tin, tiger, table*

Check that the children can name the objects before hiding them in the setting. Give the children different challenges, depending on how experienced they are at detecting initial sounds. For example:

- *'Can you find a cup in the book corner and bring it to me?'*

- *'Can you find something beginning with p in the writing area?'*

- *'Can you bring me something beginning with t?'*

- *'Can you find something beginning with b and something beginning with r?'*

As children bring the objects back, identify their initial sounds and sort them into sound groups. At the end of the activity, go through each group of items, emphasizing their initial sounds. You can also introduce the corresponding letters for some of the sounds (see **Textured letters**, pages 38–40).

★ TIPS

Hide items that link to a specific topic. For example, ask the children to find a toy, food item, vehicle beginning with …

The opportunity to move around the setting can be helpful for children who find it difficult to sit still, but you may need an assistant to help keep the child 'on task'.

I taste with my little tongue

Introduce this game once children are adept at Step 2 and moving on to Step 3 of the standard **I spy**. Gather a collection of food items beginning with different sounds. For example – **a**pple, **b**un, **c**arrot, **c**heese. Play the game as in Step 2 of **I spy with my little eye**, changing the words to *'I taste with my little tongue something beginning with …'*. Offer children a taste of the food, once you have identified its initial sound. Check for any allergies before introducing foods and never force a reluctant child to taste something. Store perishable foods in the fridge, particularly meat, dairy and cooked rice. At the end of the game, you can also introduce the corresponding letters for some of the sounds you have explored (see **Textured letters**, pages 38–40).

⭐ TIPS

Link this activity with a topic on 'Food'.

I feel with my little fingers

Make a collection of familiar objects with distinctive shapes and physical features. For example: *comb*, *doll*, *feather*, *shell*, *spoon*, *necklace*. Put two or three items in a drawstring bag and say to a child: *'Can you feel with your little fingers something beginning with …?'* Ask the child to feel the items in the bag and pick out the one that begins with the given sound. At the end of the game, you can also introduce the corresponding letters for some of the sounds you have played with (see **Textured letters**, pages 38–40)

⭐ TIPS

Choose items to link with a particular topic. For example, during autumn, put a conker, an autumn leaf, some hazel nuts and a toy squirrel in the bag.

✓ READINESS

All ages can dig for treasure in **Digging up sounds**. Help younger ones to name the objects and encourage older ones to identify the initial sound. Children need to be confident at identifying initial sounds before playing **Hunt the sound**; adapt the game for younger ones by asking them to find just a named object. **I taste with my little tongue** and **I feel with my little fingers** offer the additional challenge (and distraction) of something to taste or feel. Use them as practise and reinforcement with children who are quite adept at identifying the initial sound of a word. Children who find **I feel with my little fingers** difficult can simply pick an item from the bag to name and explore.

CURRICULUM GUIDANCE

Yellow stepping stone: *distinguish one sound from another*

Green stepping stone: *hear and say the initial sound in words …*

NLS/WORD: *hearing and identifying initial sounds in words*

Segmenting words

Once children are confident at detecting initial sounds, they can start listening out for the other phonemes that make up a simple CVC word. The process of segmenting words is a precursor to word building and writing words (see **The word basket**, pages 64–5).

For settings who are following the DfES (2004) *Playing with Sounds* approach, choose words/objects/pictures to fit in with the phoneme/grapheme correspondence groups (see **How to Use this Book**, pages 4–5).

Segmenting words with 'I spy'

Introduce all the sounds that make up a CVC word, using the familiar format of ***I spy with my little eye*** (pages 29–31). Collect a few items with simple CVC names such as *bed*, *cup* and *dog*. Say to the group '*I spy with my little eye a d-o-g*'. Ask a child to say the name of the object and then select it from the group of objects on the table.

As the children become more confident, increase the challenge by including a couple of items with one or two similar phonemes. For example:

■ *cup / cap   hat / mat   dog / dot   zip / pip   pip / pin   Ben / bin*

You can also focus on end or middle sounds:

■ Put out a *hat*, a *dog*, a *pip*, a *can* and a *mug* and say: '*I spy with my little eye something that ends with t*'.

■ Put out a *mat*, a *peg*, a *pin*, a *cot* and a *lid* and say: '*I spy with my little eye something with the middle sound a*'.

When a child has picked out the appropriate object, encourage the group to segment the whole word.

★ **TIPS**

Look out for opportunities to segment words throughout the day – '*Is everyone sitting on their m-a-t?*;' '*Charlie, can you pass me your c-u-p, please.*'; '*Put your empty carton in the b-i-n.*'

✓ **READINESS**

Segmenting the sounds in a word can be introduced once children have had some experience of detecting initial sounds.

CURRICULUM GUIDANCE

ELG: *hear and say initial and final sounds in words, and short vowel sounds within words*
NLS/WORD: *identifying … initial and final phonemes in CVC words*

More 'segmenting words' activities

The following activities offer the children further opportunities to explore the sounds that make up simple CVC words.

The end/middle sound basket

This activity is similar to ***The rhyme basket*** (pages 24–6) except that the focus is on end sounds or middle sounds. You will need the following resources:

End sounds
Groups of items or pictures with the same end sound:

> *hat, pot, cat, bat, nut,*
> *dog, bag, mug, log, pig*
> *ship, top, chip, cap, map*
> *bell, shell, hill, ball, Will*

Middle sounds
Groups of items or pictures with the same short vowel middle sounds:

> *top, log, dog, cot, mop*
> *bat, man, cap, bag, jam,*
> *leg, ted, peg, net, red*
> *cup, bug, bun, mug, pup*

Follow the same procedure as for ***The rhyme basket***, except that the children pair and sort items according to their end sounds or middle sounds, rather than their rhymes. As the children work with the items, help them to articulate all the sounds in each word.

More sound games

Digging up sounds (pages 31–2)
Bury items with CVC names. As the children dig them up, segment their names, encouraging them to join in as they become ready.

Hunt the sound (page 32)
Hide items with CVC names. Ask a child to hunt for a *c-u-p* in the book corner. Once children have become adept at segmenting CVC words, you can also ask them to find something ending with *-p* or something with the middle sound *-u-* in the book corner.

⭐ TIPS
If the children have played these games as initial sound activities, you may need to emphasize that, this time, you are focusing on the end sound/middle sound/segmenting the whole word.

Use errors positively, to reiterate the purpose of the activity – '*yes, pot begins with p like pig, but does it have the same middle sound as pig? Let's listen to the middle sound – p-i-g.*'

35

End sound puppet

This role-play activity encourages the children to correctly identify the end sound of an object's name. You will need a puppet, plus pairs of items with the same initial and middle sounds, but different end sounds. For example:

> *pig / pip   mat / man   cup / cub   bib / bin   pot / pod*
> *Ben / bed   dog / doll   cat / cap   Tom / top*

Check that the children can name the items you intend to use. Place a pair of items on the table, for example the *cat* and the *cap*. Introduce your puppet and explain that sometimes it gets a bit mixed up with its words and might need the children's help. Role play your puppet picking up the *cap* and saying '*I've got the cat*'. Wait for the children to correct the puppet, prompting them if necessary. Make sure you keep on emphasizing the end sounds of the words.

⭐ TIPS

Use names with younger children and children who find it difficult to hear the phonemes in words. Act out the puppet saying '*Hello To – To – To (To-m); hello No – No – No (No-ah)*'.

Have fun with more confident children. For example, ask them to give your puppet the *cat* and then insist that they've given you the *cap* – all the time emphasizing the end sounds and their differences.

✓ READINESS

Once the children have been introduced to segmenting CVC words, these games can be used to provide practise and reinforcement.

CURRICULUM GUIDANCE

ELG: *hear and say initial and final sounds in words, and short vowel sounds within words*
NLS/WORD: *identifying … initial and final phonemes in CVC words*

Useful Resources

My Very First Mother Goose Iona Opie and Rosemary Wells (Walker)
Traditional nursery rhyme collection.

Skip Across the Ocean Floella Benjamin (Frances Lincoln)
Collection of rhymes and lullabies from 24 countries, some in original language (with translations).
Available from: OXFAM

A wide selection of rhyme and song tapes and CDs, including songs from different countries.
Available from: The Early Learning Centre

Nursery Rhymes Pack
Ten A3 colour nursery rhyme posters, plus a Punjabi, Urdu and French rhyme. Includes activity ideas.
Available from: Practical Pre-school

Alphabet Sounds Teaching Tubs (ref. 011749)
Six objects for each letter of the alphabet.
Available from: The Consortium

Rhyming Sounds Teaching Tubs (ref. 012942)
Tubs of objects representing different rime groups.
Available from: The Consortium

See **Useful Addresses**, pages 126–7, for suppliers' contact details.

Matching Sound and Symbol 3

In this chapter ...

The activities in this chapter focus on the link between the sounds of language (phonemes) and the letters and digraphs (graphemes) that represent those sounds. The chapter is divided into four sections:

- ■ Introducing letters

- ■ Practising letters

- ■ Exploring letters

- ■ The alphabet.

Introducing letters

Once children have had plenty of experience of rhythm and rhyme, and are starting to explore the separate phonemes of spoken language, they can be introduced to the graphemes of written language.

For settings who are following the DfES *Playing with Sounds* approach, choose letters/words/objects/pictures to fit in with the phoneme/grapheme correspondence groups (see **How to Use this Book**, pages 4–5).

Textured letters

Grapheme/phoneme correspondences can be introduced as a direct follow on from exploring the initial sounds of words (see the activities in the **Initial sounds** section, Chapter 2). The ***Textured letters*** activity provides a template for linking letters and sounds. Although any letter cards can be used for the activity, textured letters enable children to trace the letter shapes with their fingers. This provides a useful preparation for later letter formation with a writing implement.

Resources

✓ The letter shapes *a–z*, *ch*, *sh* and *th*, cut from a textured material such as sandpaper, velvet or felt and glued onto boards or cards. These can be hand-made, using letter templates, or purchased (see **Useful resources**, page 54).

Choose whichever letter style you wish to introduce to your children. Some settings prefer print, others introduce cursive letters as a prelude to later joined-up handwriting.

Introducing the textured letters

Choose two or three letters corresponding with sounds that you have been exploring through *I Spy* (pages 29–31) and other sound detection activities. Alternatively, choose letters from the children's names or the names of favourite storybook characters. If possible, go for letters with contrasting shapes and sounds, for example *a* and *t* rather than *d* and *b*.

■ Show the children one of your chosen letters and say: *'this letter makes the sound …'*.

■ Ask the children to help you think of other words beginning with the same sound.

■ Show the children how to feel the letter in the way in which it is written, and invite each child in the group to have a turn.

■ Encourage the children to say the sound represented by the letter as they feel it.

■ Help the children to find the letter in their name cards or the name of a familiar storybook character.

■ Repeat the process with the other letters.

⭐ TIPS

You can also use the initial letters from items linked to a particular topic. Show the children a word card or find the word in a book, identify the initial sound and introduce the corresponding textured letter.

Exploring the textured letters

Once the children are able to associate a letter with its sound, set lots of little challenges to reinforce their new knowledge:

■ *'Put the letter **a** under your chair.'*

■ *'Can you hide the letter **s** in the book corner for Tara to find?'*

■ *'Can you find the letter **g** in "Mr Gumpy's Outing"?'*

⭐ TIPS

Keep reminding the children to feel the letter in the way it is written and repeat its sound.

Follow this up by looking for the letter in books, notices and other printed literature. Provide lots of active challenges for children who find it difficult to sit still. If necessary, ask an assistant to help focus the child on the task.

Before looking for a letter in a particular book, check that the print has a reasonably close correspondence to the textured letters – watch out for *a* and *g* in particular.

Assessing knowledge

For assessment purposes, see how well the children can associate the letters with their sounds:

■ Point to one of the letters without mentioning the sound it makes.

■ Ask a child: *'what sound does this letter make?'*

■ If the child does not know, simply revert to the previous stage (***Exploring the textured letters***), where you name the letter (*'Can you give me the letter c?'*).

⭐ TIPS

This process does not have to last very long. Keep things light-hearted and avoid making the children feel that they are being 'tested'.

Introduce Braille at a later stage to give children an experience of other forms of print.

✓ READINESS

Once children can identify the initial sound of a word during activities such as ***I spy*** (pages 29–31), you can start introducing the corresponding letter.

> **CURRICULUM GUIDANCE**
>
> **Green stepping stone:** *hear and say the initial sound in words and know which letters represent some of the sounds*
> **ELG:** *link sounds to letters … sounding the letters of the alphabet*
> **NLS/WORD:** *knowledge of grapheme/phoneme correspondences through: reading letters that represent the sounds a–z, ch, sh, th*

Letter aids

Although the textured letters are ideal for introducing letters, there are lots of further resources that can help to reinforce sound/letter links. The following can be used both in organized games and during independent play.

Letter flags

To make paper flags, you will need:

- ✓ Long rectangles of thin card
- ✓ Letter templates, preferably in the same script as the textured letters
- ✓ Marker pen
- ✓ PVA craft glue
- ✓ Chopsticks or lengths of thin wooden dowelling.

Use the template to write a letter towards the left-hand side and the right-hand side of the card. Spread lots of PVA glue all over the underside of the card. Fold the card in half around the length of dowelling so that the two sides are firmly stuck together, with the dowelling acting as a flagstick.

 TIPS

Check that the flag is well glued so that it can withstand being handled. For a stronger flag, use a fabric such as felt.

Letter washing line

A washing line is a quick, easy way to make alphabet displays. String the line along a wall and peg up letters. These can include cut-out letters, letter cards and letters set alongside a corresponding picture. Use a favourite story that has lots of items, for example Eric Carle's *The Very Hungry Caterpillar* (Puffin). Ask the children to draw pictures of items from the story, such as *the caterpillar*, *an apple*, *a pear*, *the sun*, *a leaf* and so on. Identify the initial sounds of the items, match with their letters and peg up on the washing line.

Letter puppets and mittens

Puppets or mittens with fabric letter shapes can be used for letter role-play games. For example, you can use letter puppets to play a game such as **Finger folk sounds** (pages 27–8). Make a few hand puppets from felt, glue Velcro hooks to the front of the puppet and cut out the letter shapes from felt. Attach your chosen letter to the front of the puppet. The felt letters should stick to the Velcro hooks by themselves, but you can add strength by gluing Velcro fur to the backs of the letters. Felt letters can also be attached to mittens.

Alphabet books

Alphabet books play an essential role in helping young children to associate letters and sounds. Introduce lots of different examples and encourage the children to look at them independently. When you are exploring a particular letter, look at that letter in your collection of alphabet books and ask the children to find the letter for themselves.

⭐ TIPS

Check that the pictures in the alphabet books are phonetically appropriate at this early stage. For example, *igloo* is a better choice than *ice cream* for the letter *i*; the most useful way to represent *x* is to have a word ending with *x*, such as *fox*.

✓ READINESS

Letter flags, ***Letter puppets***, ***Letter mittens*** and ***Alphabet books*** can be used by any age group. Even if the children cannot yet link a letter with its sound, they will still benefit from being exposed to the letter shapes through playing with these resources.

CURRICULUM GUIDANCE

Green stepping stone: *hear and say the initial sound in words and know which letters represent some of the sounds*

ELG: *link sounds to letters … sounding the letters of the alphabet*

NLS/WORD: *knowledge of grapheme/phoneme correspondences through: reading letters that represent the sounds a–z, ch, sh, th*

Practising letters

Once children are starting to associate sounds with their letter symbols, it is important to give them lots of reinforcement in the form of different games and activities.

For settings who are following the DfES (2004) *Playing with Sounds* approach, choose letters/words/objects/pictures to fit in with the phoneme/grapheme correspondence groups (see **How to Use this Book**, pages 4–5).

Activities from 'The Sounds of Language'

Many of the games and activities from Chapter 2 (**The Sounds of Language**) can be adapted to use letters as well as sounds. This has the advantage of introducing something new (the letter symbols) within a familiar context.

I spy with letters

(See pages 29–31)
Use the textured letters as your starting point. Hold up a letter and say '*I spy with my little eye something that begins with this letter*'. If children are only just beginning to associate sounds and letters, you can say the sound as you hold up the letter.

Digging up letters

(See pages 31–2)
Bury plastic, wooden and foam letters in the sand box. When the children have dug up a letter, challenge them to identify its sound and find a matching letter in the setting – in a book, a notice, as a ***Letter flag***.

The letter basket

This activity follows a similar format to *The rhyme basket* (See pages 24–6). Fill a basket with a selection of familiar objects and gather together the corresponding textured letters. For example, a *teddy* and the letter *t*. Set out the textured letters on one large floor mat and place the letter basket on a second floor mat. Ask a child to pick an object, identify its initial sound and find the matching letter. The object and letter can then be placed together on the mat. Put each letter in context by writing the name of the object with the letter highlighted in a different colour.

⭐ TIPS

Link with a particular topic by choosing associated items. For example, 'Toys': *doll* for *d*, *teddy* for *t*, *puzzle* for *p*.

The use of interesting objects can help children to engage in the game, although do make sure that the object does not distract them from the main purpose of the activity.

✓ READINESS

To begin with, simply introduce the letter along with the sound when playing *I spy* and *Digging up sounds*. Once the children have had some experience with letter/sound correspondences, you can challenge them to make the link for themselves. To play *The letter basket* independently, the children need to be confident at identifying the initial sound of an object and associating a sound with its corresponding letter.

CURRICULUM GUIDANCE

Green stepping stone: *hear and say the initial sound in words and know which letters represent some of the sounds*

ELG: *link sounds to letters … sounding the letters of the alphabet*

NLS/WORD: *knowledge of grapheme/phoneme correspondences through: reading letters that represent the sounds a–z, ch, sh, th*

On the mat!

This activity encourages the children to identify the initial sound of an object and decide whether that sound links with a particular letter symbol.

Resources

✓ A large floor mat

✓ Groups of familiar objects made up of two or three items with CVC names and beginning with the same sound. For example:

bed, bat, bun
cat, cup, can
pig, pot, pen
mat, mug, mop

✓ A set of large letter cards, corresponding to names of the objects.

The activity

■ Seat the children in a wide circle and place a large floor mat in the centre of the circle.

■ Give each of the children an object to hold and ask them to identify the initial sound of their object.

■ Explain to the group that you are going to hold up a letter card. The children must then listen very carefully and when you say '*on the mat*', any child who has an object beginning with that letter must run to the mat with his or her object.

■ Ensure that all the children get a turn at running to the mat.

■ Exchange objects so that the children can work with a different initial sound and letter.

⭐ TIPS

Avoid making the children feel pressured. Go through the initial sound of some of the items on the mat, but play down any objects that do not match the letter you held up.

Heighten the excitement by pausing before saying '*on the mat*'. This encourages the children to listen carefully and adds to the fun of the activity.

Take photos of the items, ask children to match the pictures with letter cards and peg them to the **Letter washing line** (page 41).

Ask an assistant to support children who find it hard to listen and might miss the moment to run to the mat.

✓ READINESS

Children need to have had prior experience of the sounds and letters you select for this game. You may need to practise the game a few times, before the children become familiar with it.

CURRICULUM GUIDANCE

Green stepping stones: *hear and say the initial sound in words and know which letters represent some of the sounds*

ELG: *link sounds to letters ... sounding the letters of the alphabet*

NLS/WORD: *knowledge of grapheme/phoneme correspondences through: reading letters that represent the sounds a–z, ch, sh, th*

Letter identification games

These games encourage the children to practise and reinforce their knowledge of sound and letter links. Most of the games encourage the children to identify a given letter within a CVC word. As part of the activity, you can also model the process of sounding out/blending sounds to read the whole word. These games can be played in conjunction with **The reading basket** (pages 78–80).

Circle game letters

- Make a circle of chairs.

- Gather together some CVC word cards containing the letters you wish to highlight, plus the corresponding letter flags.

- Blu-tak a word card to the back of each chair and seat the children on the chairs.

- Give a child a letter flag, for example *b*, and ask her to identify its sound.

- Sing the following to the tune of *Twinkle, Twinkle, Little Star*:

  > *Hannah is holding a 'b' in her hand*
  > *Is there another 'b' for Hannah to find?*

- Ask Hannah to walk around the outside of the group until she finds a word card containing her letter on the back of a chair, for example *bun*.

- Ask her to bring the word card and letter flag to the front of the group and check that the word *bun* contains the letter.

- Sound out the word – *b-u-n* – and blend the phonemes to read the word.

- Replace the word card on the back of the chair and give the child sitting on that chair the next turn (seat Hannah on the now vacant chair).

- Continue until all the children have had a turn.

⭐ **TIPS**

To ensure that every child gets their turn, have a list of the letters and tick them off as they are matched.

Stepping stone letters

- Choose three or four sounds/letters.

- Make some large CVC word cards beginning with your chosen letters, with the initial letter written in a different colour.

- ■ Chalk the letters onto the playground or write them on large pieces of card to Blu-tak to the floor of your setting.

- ■ Play some music and challenge the children to dance around the letters without stepping on them.

- ■ Stop the music and hold up a large word card, for example *fan*.

- ■ Sound out the word – *f-a-n* – and blend the sounds to read the word.

- ■ Identify the initial sound/letter *f* and ask the children to find a letter *f* to stand on.

- ■ Help each child to position themselves so that they are looking at the letter the right way up (if you have a large group, get an assistant to help).

- ■ Continue with other words and letters.

- ■ As the children get the idea, you can leave them to identify the initial letter for themselves.

- ■ When the children are confident at associating sounds and letters, dispense with holding up a word card and simply give a sound.

⭐ TIPS

Have several examples of each letter on the floor, to avoid collisions.

Ask an assistant to support those children who find it difficult to stand still when the music stops.

Traditional games

Traditional group games such as **Lotto**, **Bingo** and **Palmanism** can all be used to help children establish letter/sound correspondences.

Letter lotto
You will need:

- ✓ Several cards (approximately 18 cm × 12 cm) divided into six equal sections, with a different CVC word written on each section. Each word should have one of its letters in a different colour. Check that no lotto card has the same letter highlighted more than once. For example: *dog/cap/pig/mug/hen/zip*.

- ✓ 3 sets of letter cards for the 26 letters of the alphabet, slightly smaller than the sections on the large lotto card and preferably a different colour from the lotto cards.

- ✓ A drawstring bag.

Give each child a large lotto card. Ask a child to pick a letter card from the drawstring bag and identify its sound. If they have the letter highlighted in one of their lotto card words, they can place it on top of the corresponding section. As you play the game, sound out the words and encourage the children to join in.

Letter bingo

You will need the same resources as for **Lotto**, plus large coloured counters. Give each child a lotto card and a selection of counters. Pick a letter card from the drawstring bag and show it to the group. Those children with that letter highlighted in a word on their card can place a counter on top. The first child to fill their card shouts '*Bingo!*'

Letter palmanism

You will need:

✓ Two sets of letter cards with identical backs.

Place the two sets of letter cards face down. Ask a child to turn over two cards. If the letters match, the child can keep the pair.

★ TIPS

For **Palmanism**, substitute picture cards for one of the letter sets. Check that the backs of the picture cards are identical. Link with a particular topic by choosing associated pictures. For example, 'Fruits': *peach* for *p*, *kiwi* for *k*, *lemon* for *l*.

The structured nature of these games can be useful for children who benefit from routine and repetitive activities.

✓ READINESS

Children should have had some experience of matching the sounds and letters you plan to use in the games. For **Traditional games**, the child also needs to be able to follow the rules of a game and take turns. Encourage children who are ready to help you sound out/blend the sounds to read the words.

CURRICULUM GUIDANCE

Green stepping stone (linking sounds and letters): *know which letters represent some of the sounds*

ELG: *link sounds to letters … sounding the letters of the alphabet*

Blue stepping stone (reading): *understand the concept of a word*

Green stepping stone (reading): *begin to recognise some familiar words*

NLS/WORD: *knowledge of grapheme/phoneme correspondences through: reading letters that represent the sounds a–z, ch, sh, th*

Exploring letters

The activities in this section encourage children to use their creativity in exploring different aspects of sounds and letters.

Sorting letters

This activity introduces children to the many different font styles to be found within books, magazines and other printed literature.

Resources

- ✓ Newspapers, magazines, comics, leaflets, brochures
- ✓ Letter resources such as magnetic letters, foam letters, letter cards, the textured letters, letter flags, postcards of illuminated letters
- ✓ 29 heavy duty envelopes
- ✓ Large sheets of card
- ✓ PVA craft glue
- ✓ Black marker pen.

The activity

Make a letter sorting chart by writing each letter of the alphabet plus *sh*, *ch* and *th* on the fronts of the envelopes, and sticking them to the sheets of card. Give each child a different letter to find. Help them to search for their letter in small chunks of text cut from magazines, newspapers and leaflets. Talk about the different print styles – which do the children like best, which letters look most like the textured letters or letter flags? Help the children to cut out their letters and slip them inside the corresponding letter envelope. When you have finished the activity, count through the letters. Which envelope has the most letters and which has the least? Did the children notice that it was easy to find letters such as *e* and *s* and harder to find letters such as *x* and *z*? Ask the children to decorate the chart and continue finding letters to put in the envelopes.

★ TIPS

Give extra support where necessary by choosing a common letter such as *e* or *t* and giving a child a single line of print to look through.

Include a symbol sorting activity using different scripts, such as Chinese. If possible, find a native speaker of the language to help you prepare the activity.

If the envelopes start to show signs of wear, put sticky tape around the edges and check that they are firmly glued to the chart.

✓ **READINESS**

Ideally, children should be familiar with a letter before exploring it in different font styles.

> **CURRICULUM GUIDANCE**
>
> **Yellow stepping stone:** *show interest in … print in books and print in the environment*
>
> **Green stepping stone:** *hear and say the initial sound in words and know which letters represent some of the sounds*
>
> **ELG:** *explore and experiment with … texts*
>
> **ELG:** *link sounds to letters … sounding the letters of the alphabet*
>
> **NLS/WORD (phonics):** *knowledge of grapheme/phoneme correspondences: through reading letters that represent the sounds a–z, ch, sh, th*

Letter posters

This activity encourages children to explore many different elements of sounds and letters, in order to make a poster to display in the setting.

The activity

Choose a letter such as *b*. Cut out a large *b* shape from a sheet of card. Ask the children to help you think of objects whose names begin with *b* – *box, bag, brick, berry, Ben*. Go through magazines and cut out pictures of relevant items. Ask the children to draw pictures of *b* objects, giving them smallish pieces of paper to work on so that their drawings will fit onto your large *b*. Tour the setting with the children, finding *b* objects to photograph. Go through magazines, cutting out different samples of the letter *b*. Decorate the letter shape by sticking on the pictures, photos, drawings and print. Include some real objects; for example, stick on a small cardboard *box*. Include a photo of any child whose name begins with *b*. Add pictures of favourite storybook characters whose names begin with *b*. Write the name of each picture or object, highlighting the initial letter in a different colour. If certain colours begin with your letter, use them to paint the letter shape – for example, *blue, brown* and *black*. Encourage older/able children to come up with their own ideas for a letter poster.

⭐ **TIPS**

If you have too many bits and pieces to fit onto the letter outline, glue everything to a large sheet of card.

✓ **READINESS**

Children of any age can join in decorating letters as an art activity. To gain fully from the literacy element of the activity, children need to be familiar with the letter/sound link and able to recognize the letter in different font styles.

CURRICULUM GUIDANCE

Yellow stepping stone: *show interest in … print in books and print in the environment*
ELG: *explore and experiment with … texts*
ELG: *link sounds to letters … sounding the letters of the alphabet*
NLS/WORD: *knowledge of grapheme/phoneme correspondences: through reading letters that represent the sounds a–z, ch, sh, th*

A *letter week*

This activity focuses on a particular sound/letter association over a period of time. It brings together all the different ways of learning about and exploring letters.

The activity

Start off by choosing the letter you wish to focus on. Get the children to help you compose a note for home, asking carers to help their child find items beginning with the letter. Set up a table display for the items. Add the textured letter, letter flag, letter puppet and any other letter resources such as foam and magnetic letters. Display some alphabet books open at the relevant page. During the week, make a letter poster for the relevant letter, or start an alphabet scrap book to build up throughout the year. Do printing activities using potato and sponge cuts in the shape of the letter. For children who are starting to write letters (page 59), put out blackboards, chalk, paper and pencils along with the appropriate textured letter. If you play **Circle game letters** (page 45) and other games, make sure you flag up your 'letter of the week'. Choose the letter/sound of the week for playing **Action tongue twisters** (page 28) and **Have you any wellies?** (page 26). Pick out all the children whose names begin with the letter at register time. Challenge the children to look out for examples of the letter in unexpected places:

- Write the letter on snack-time paper mats and cups.

- Use writing icing to decorate biscuits or muffins.

- Arrange apple chunks or grapes in the shape of the letter on a large platter.

- Thread a ribbon in the shape of the letter through wire netting in the playground.

- Write the letter in non-permanent marker pen on the mirror in the cloakroom.

- Put stickers with the letter above certain children's pegs.

- Bury cut-out card letters in the sand box for the children to dig up.

Ask the children to make a group list of all the different places where they have found the letter throughout the week. Keep on reiterating the link between the letter and its sound, and look out for words beginning with or containing the letter.

⭐ **TIPS**

Unless your memory is good, keep a list of where you have hidden all the different letter samples so that you can direct children towards any that remain unfound by the end of the week.

Encourage older/able children to participate in planning and preparing the **Letter week** activities. For example, they can hide letters in the setting for you and the other children to find.

✓ **READINESS**

Children can participate in this activity at whatever level they have reached. Younger ones can simply focus on the initial sounds of the objects they have brought in and join in making a letter poster and letter prints as an art activity. Although they may not yet have been introduced to letters, they will still benefit from being exposed to the letter shape. For children who have been introduced to letters, the activity will help to reinforce their knowledge of the letter/sound association and some of the words which contain that letter.

CURRICULUM GUIDANCE

Yellow stepping stone: *show interest in … print in books and print in the environment*

ELG: *explore and experiment with … texts*

ELG: *link sounds to letters … sounding the letters of the alphabet*

NLS/WORD: *knowledge of grapheme/phoneme correspondences: through reading letters that represent the sounds a–z, ch, sh, th*

The alphabet

The activities in this section introduce letters in the form of capitals (upper case), letter names and the order of the alphabet.

Capital letters

Once children are getting to grips with sound/letter associations, you can start introducing them to capital letter shapes and the name of the letter (Ay) as opposed to the sound it makes (***a***pple).

Resources

- ✓ 52 white cards, approximately 8 cm × 8 cm

- ✓ Upper and lower case letter templates (optional)

- ✓ Black marker pen

- ✓ Laminator or clear sticky-backed plastic.

The activity

Make a set of upper case (capital letter) cards and a matching set of lower case cards. Choose two or three letters, preferably the initial letters from some of the children's names. Explain to the children that, today, you are going to find out something new about letters and sounds. Show them the lower case card for one of the letters, identify the sound it makes and then introduce the upper case letter. Explain to the children: '*This makes the sound **a**, but its name is **Ay**.*' Show the children the capital letters at the start of the appropriate name card. Repeat the process for the other two letters.

As the children get to know the letters as capitals, introduce different activities to reinforce their knowledge:

- Look out for samples of capital letters in the setting and outside – signs and notices, the initial letters of names in the register.

- Look through books for capital letters. Focus in particular on titles, the start of sentences and the names of the characters.

- Find and cut out samples of capitals to add to the letter sorting chart (see **Sorting letters**, pages 48–9).

- Select a few upper case and corresponding lower case letters and ask children to match them. They can then be pegged up in pairs on the **Letter washing line** (page 41).

- Make felt capital letters to attach to the **Letter puppets** (page 41). Use them to play **Finger folk sounds** (pages 27–8) and other games.

- Make capital letter potato cuts and string blocks for printing activities.

- Cut out large capital letters from thin card for children to decorate with paint, printing and collage.

- Introduce capital letter puzzles (see **Useful resources**, page 54).

- Many alphabet books show both upper and lower case letters. Look at these with the children and challenge them to pick out and name the capital letters.

✓ READINESS

Children can start learning the names of letters and upper case letter shapes once they are confident at linking lower case letters and sounds.

CURRICULUM GUIDANCE

ELG: *link sounds to letters, <u>naming</u> and sounding the letters of the alphabet*
NLS/WORD: *knowledge of grapheme/phoneme correspondence through: sounding and <u>naming</u> each letter of the alphabet in lower and <u>upper case</u>*

Learning the alphabet

Once children have learnt the letter names and capital letter shapes, they can be introduced to alphabetical order.

The activities

Choose some appropriate tunes for singing the alphabet and gradually teach them to the group. Once children can sing the alphabet, play games to help reinforce their knowledge of alphabetical order:

- ■ Give each child a capital letter card and ask them to hold up their card as you slowly sing the alphabet.

- ■ Encourage the children to put the set of capital letter cards in order. Ask one child to find *A*, another *B* and so on. As the children become more confident, they can do this by themselves.

- ■ Use alphabet books to reinforce the order of the letters – can the children tell you which letter will be on the next page?

- ■ Look through dictionaries and encyclopaedias and show the children how the pages are arranged in alphabetical order.

✓ READINESS

Children should have been introduced to the names of the letters and be able to recognize capital letters before going on to learn alphabetical order.

CURRICULUM GUIDANCE

ELG: *link sounds to letters, <u>naming</u> and sounding the letters of the alphabet*

NLS/WORD: *knowledge of grapheme/phoneme correspondences through: sounding and <u>naming</u> each letter of the alphabet in lower and <u>upper case</u>*

NLS/WORD: *alphabetic and phonic knowledge through: understanding alphabetical order through alphabet books, rhymes and songs*

Useful Resources

Global Alphabet books, including **A is for Africa**, **C is for China** and **I is for India** (Frances Lincoln Publishers)
Available from: OXFAM

Alphabet Pack
Alphabet frieze made up of loose-leaf A4 posters, with photocopiable activity sheets for parents on the back.
Available from: Practical Pre-school

Tactile Sandpaper Letters
Print (ref. 13290)
Cursive (ref. 13382)
Capitals (ref. 13383)
Available from: Philip and Tacey

Lower Case Magnetic Letters (ref. 010076) tub of 288; **Upper Case Magnetic Letters** (ref. 010077) tub of 288; **Framed Magnetic Board** (ref. 010079) pack of 6; **Foam Letters and Numbers** (ref. 008997) tub of 1,500; **Lower Case Wooden Letters** (ref. 011193) pack of 50; **Upper Case Wooden Letters** (ref. 011192) pack of 50.
Available from: The Consortium

Alphabet Puzzle Trays (ref. 006645) wooden inset puzzles, lower case and ABC turtle.
Available from: The Consortium

Alphabet Washing Line (ref. E58491) includes line, pegs and sets of lower case, upper case and alphabet picture cards; **Alphabet Bean Bags** (ref. G24652) bean bags with upper case letters on one side and lower case on the other; **abc Wallhanging** (ref. E58519) fabric wallhanging with lower case letters and soft toys.
Available from: NES Arnold

See **Useful Addresses**, pages 126–7, for suppliers' contact details.

Becoming a Writer

In this chapter ...

This chapter focuses on the many different elements that come together to make up the act of writing. The chapter is divided into three sections:

- ■ Pre-writing activities

- ■ Handwriting

- ■ Content.

Pre-writing activities

Before children reach the stage of actually writing letters and words, they need to develop the muscular strength and co-ordination required to hold and control a writing implement.

Developing muscular strength and co-ordination

These are just a few of the many activities that help to develop controlled arm movements and muscular strength in the three writing digits (index and middle fingers and thumb).

Knobbed puzzles and peg boards

Provide plenty of knobbed wooden puzzles and peg boards. Although children will tend to hold the whole puzzle piece, encourage them to grip the knob with the three writing digits whenever possible. Set them a challenge – '*can you put the puzzle piece in the puzzle like this?*'

Sprinkling sand and glitter

Show the children how to pick up sand, glitter, dried flowers or rice in the thumb and index finger. Sprinkle onto glue as part of an art activity.

⭐ TIPS
Make sure the children do not rub sand or glitter into the eyes.

Threading

Threading a lace through holes punched into card helps to develop controlled hand and arm movements. Gripping the lace helps to develop strength in the index finger and thumb.

Using tweezers

Picking things up with tweezers strengthens the pincer grip (index finger and thumb) and involves a high degree of hand/eye co-ordination. Show the children how to use the tweezers to transfer dried peas from one bowl to another.

⭐ TIPS
As children become more adept at using tweezers, challenge them to pick up small grains such as rice.

Ribbon patterns

For this activity, you will need several lengths of ribbon, about 1 m long and approximately 1.5 cm wide. Demonstrate how to wave the ribbon to make patterns in the air. Encourage the children to make large-scale movements that reflect the shapes of writing – up and down, side to side, round and round, and wavy arm movements.

⭐ TIPS
Encourage the children to wave their ribbons in time to some rhythmic music.

✓ READINESS
Knobbed puzzles and ***Sprinkling sand and glitter*** can be introduced to children of any age. The children will gradually become more adept at these activities as their strength and co-ordination develops. ***Using tweezers*** and ***Ribbon patterns*** are more demanding. Introduce tweezers once children have sufficient strength in the index finger and thumb. Introduce waving ribbons once children have some control over large arm movements.

CURRICULUM GUIDANCE

Yellow stepping stones: *engage in activities requiring hand/eye co-ordination and use one-handed tools and equipment*
Blue stepping stone: *manipulate objects with increasing control*

Mark making and patterning

Children need lots of opportunity to explore mark making and creating patterns. Gradually, their explorations on paper will take on a more 'writing-like' quality and they will start to assign meaning to their marks.

Using writing materials

Apart from modelling writing and providing a print-rich environment, offering free access to writing materials is the single most important way of encouraging the development of writing. See Chapter 1 (**The Setting**) for suggestions on how to set up a writing area.

⭐ TIPS

Encourage the children to talk about their mark making. Avoid asking them *'what is it?'* or *'what does it say?'* – but do listen out for indications that they are assigning meanings to their marks.

Painting/Wet cornflour

Even the youngest children can create striking marks and images with paint. The big format of the painting paper encourages large movements, while holding the paint brush helps to develop muscular strength and hand/eye co-ordination. Finger painting and messy play with wet cornflour are also valuable activities. Encourage the children to make patterns that link with letter formation – vertical/horizontal lines, zig-zags, loops, wavy lines, circles (anticlockwise to reflect correct formation for letters such as *d*).

⭐ TIPS

Some children don't like getting their hands painty. Try painting sponges as a 'halfway point' between fingers and a paintbrush.

Playdough and clay

Give the children lots of implements for mark making in playdough or damp clay – lego bricks, cotton reels, glue spatulas, pastry cutters. Manipulating modelling materials is also great for developing muscular strength and co-ordination.

⭐ TIPS

These activities can be very calming for children who are restless or over-stimulated by their environment.

✓ READINESS

Children can start exploring activities such as ***Using writing materials***, ***Painting/Wet cornflour*** and ***Playdough*** as soon as they arrive in your setting. Introduce writing related patterns once children can produce a controlled line. Creating patterns with the hands in finger paint is easier than using a paintbrush. Clay is tougher to manipulate than playdough; save it for older ones with larger hands and greater muscular strength.

CURRICULUM GUIDANCE

Yellow stepping stone (writing): *draw and paint, sometimes giving meaning to marks*

Blue stepping stone (writing): *ascribe meaning to marks*

Yellow stepping stones (handwriting): *engage in activities requiring hand/eye co-ordination* and *use one-handed tools and equipment*

Blue stepping stones (handwriting): *draw lines and circles using gross motor movement and manipulate objects with increasing control*

Green stepping stone (handwriting): *begin to use anticlockwise movement and retrace vertical lines*

Handwriting

Writing letters and words follows on from linking sounds and letters, learning the letter shapes and developing co-ordinated hand movements. Provide lots of opportunity for the children to explore writing materials and watch as their 'writing-like' marks gradually evolve into recognizable letters. If you want to give a child a little nudge towards writing, you can also introduce the following activities.

Writing letters

These activities enable the children to practise letter formation, prior to using a pencil.

Writing letters in air

Seat a small group of children so that you are all facing the same direction. Choose one of the ***Textured letters*** (pages 38–40) and ask the children to identify its sound. Look for the letter in name cards and other handwritten literature. Give each child a turn at tracing the letter with the fingers before 'writing' it in the air. Introduce a letterbox and a feely bag containing textured or cut-out letters. Ask a child to pick a letter from the bag, draw it in the air and then post it into the letterbox. Introduce this activity at odd moments throughout the day – during lunch or as a part of taking the register.

⭐ TIPS

Link writing letters with a favourite story or nursery rhyme. Find the initial letter of a character's name in the book and practise writing the letter.

Encourage children with co-ordination difficulties to make simple up and down and circular movements with the arm.

While children are still establishing left- or right-handedness, let them write in the air with both hands.

As the children become more familiar with the letter shapes, set them some challenges: *'Can you write a huge/tiny p in the air? Can you see which letter I am writing …?'*

Writing letters in sand

Writing letters in sand can be introduced while children are playing in the sand box. Put some sand into a flat tray and show the children how to write a letter with the index finger. Show them how to shake the tray gently to make the sand smooth again.

Writing letters with chalk and pencil

If a child is not spontaneously starting to write letters during free exploration with writing materials, try introducing the activity. Choose a **Textured letter** from the child's name. Introduce, as with the **Writing letters in air** activity, and find the letter in the child's name card. Explain to the child: *'I'm going to show you how to write the letter p, just like the p in your name.'* Write the letter with chalk on a blackboard. Offer the child a turn and encourage him or her to repeat writing the letter. Continue with other letters from the child's name. As the child becomes more confident, progress to a pencil and paper.

⭐ TIPS

Encourage children to grip the pencil between their thumb and forefinger so that it rests on the middle finger.

An unconventional grip is only a problem if it is impeding the child's writing. As long as children are enjoying mark making and developing their writing skills, leave well alone. If intervention is needed, try triangular pencils or pencil grips. Monitor the child carefully, to make sure the pencil is being correctly used. Check that the child is not gripping it too tightly.

✓ READINESS

Before **Writing letters in air** and **Writing letters in sand**, children need to have been introduced to the letter shapes and, ideally, have experience of tracing textured letters with the fingers. Young children should never be pushed to write letters and words. If you do introduce letter writing with chalk and pencils as a planned activity, check that the child has had plenty of experience with letter/sound links, tracing textured letters, writing in the air, activities to develop muscular control and hand/eye co-ordination and free exploration of writing materials. If a child has no interest in writing letters, even when shown, leave it and try again at a later date.

CURRICULUM GUIDANCE

Green stepping stone (handwriting): *begin to form recognisable letters*

ELG: *use a pencil and hold it effectively to form recognisable letters, most of which are correctly formed*

NLS/WORD: *knowledge of grapheme/phoneme correspondences through: writing each letter in response to each sound: a–z, ch, sh, th*

NLS/WORD: *use a comfortable and efficient pencil grip; produce a controlled line which supports letter formation; write letters using the correct sequence of movements*

Exploring letter shapes

These activities focus on different letter shapes and the common ways in which certain letters are formed.

Sorting letter shapes

Decide how you are going to sort a set of cut-out letters. For example: letters with tails (*f, j, p, y*) and letters with arms sticking up (*b, d, h, k*). As an alternative, use the writing direction of the letter: anticlockwise (*a, c, d*); downwards from the top (*b, l, j*); slantwise (*v, w, x*). Your groupings will vary depending on whether you are using a cursive or print style of letter.

- Pick one of the letters, for example *y*.

- Point out how its tail hangs down and ask the children to find some other letters with tails.

- Group the tailed letters on a mat.

- Choose another letter type to focus on and continue the activity until all the letters have been sorted.

- Make the activity fun – talk about *b* having a big fat tummy because he has eaten too much breakfast.

- Use mathematical and expressive language to describe the shapes – *o* is round, *l* is a straight line, *c* is curved, *i* has a dot, *s* is like a curly snake.

⭐ **TIPS**

Give the children just a small number of letters to sort through and include several examples of the letter group for them to find.

For children who tend to invert or reverse letters, focus on correct positioning by helping them to peg up cut-out card letters on the ***Letter washing line*** (page 41).

At a later stage, explore different scripts such as Chinese. Find someone with knowledge of the language to help you prepare the activity.

Letter shape gymnastics

Many of the letter shapes can be created using parts of the body. Before trying each 'letter gymnastic', use a large letter card to remind the children of the letter shape.

- Stretch up your arms and stick out your tummy like *b*.

- Curl your index finger and thumb to make a *c*.

- Stretch up your arm like *h*.

- Create an *i* by placing one child stretched out on the floor to make the straight line and a second child curled into a ball to make the dot.

- Stand up straight and stick out your arms at angles to make a *k*.

- Make your whole body into a tall, straight *l*.

- Ask two children to make bridges with their bodies and place them side by side to make an *m*.

- Join the tips of your index fingers and thumbs to make a round *o*.

- Stretch out your arms to make a *v*.

- Hang your arm down and curl up your hand to make a curly tail like *y*.

⭐ **TIPS**

As you create the different shapes, highlight the features of a particular letter – '*i has a dot, l is a straight line*'.

The physically active nature of this activity is useful for children who find it hard to sit still – but don't expect them to hold their letter shape position for too long!

Placing letters on a line

Once children are confident at writing letters, you can start to introduce the correct positioning of letters on a line. Choose some cut-out letters with tails that hang down below the line (*j*, *p*), some letters with arms that stick up (*d*, *h*) and some letters that simply rest on the line (*c*, *o*). Show the children how to place the letters on a lined card or felt mat with embroidered lines. Use the same language as you introduced during the **Sorting letter shapes** activity; for *b*, emphasize that its '*big fat tummy*' sits on the line; for tailed letters such as *y*, emphasize that '*its curly tail*' hangs down below the line. As children become ready, encourage them to write some of the letters and simple words on lined blackboards, whiteboards or paper.

⭐ **TIPS**

Before embarking on this activity, check that the lines on your card or mat are the correct width to accommodate your cut-out letters.

✓ READINESS

Before being introduced to **Sorting letter shapes** and **Letter shape gymnastics**, children need to have had some experience of letters through activities such as tracing textured letters, air writing and writing letters in sand. For **Letter shape gymnastics**, children also need to be able to co-ordinate the whole body – although exploring the features of the letter is more important than recreating its shape. Children need to be confident at writing letters and simple words, before being introduced to **Placing letters on a line**.

CURRICULUM GUIDANCE

Green stepping stone: *begin to form recognisable letters*

ELG: *use a pencil and hold it effectively to form recognisable letters, most of which are correctly formed*

NLS/WORD: *write letters using the correct sequence of movements*

NLS/TEXT: *through shared writing: understand how letters are formed*

Content

The main purpose of writing is to communicate, and children need to discover that writing is a useful means of recording their thoughts, ideas and messages. Introduce lots of activities that focus on the content of writing and try out different writing formats such as lists, captions and labels.

Writing names

For most children, their name is the first word that they learn to recognize and write. Names make a good starting point for writing – partly because they are so familiar and partly because the ability to write one's own name helps a child to operate smoothly within the setting.

Resources

✓ A name card holder, with pockets for each name and photos attached to the front of the pockets so that children can find their name cards.

✓ A laminated name card for each child, with the name handwritten on one side and printed on the other (use a capital letter at the start).

✓ Cut-out letters.

✓ Writing materials such as chalk, blackboard, pencils and paper.

The activities

Show the children how to find their names in the name chart and encourage them to explore and use their written names whenever possible:

■ Working with small groups of children, help them to select the cut-out letters that spell their names and put them in the correct order.

■ Help the children to peg up painted self-portraits and their names in cut-out card letters on the **Letter washing line** (page 41).

■ Make lists of name cards as part of organizing the day. For example, write on a large sheet of paper: '*These children can use the climbing frame today*', with the appropriate names attached to the paper with Blu-tak.

■ Encourage children to place their name cards in a queuing system for popular activities.

■ When you sing songs that use the children's names, ask them to hold up their name cards.

■ Encourage the children to watch whenever you write their names.

■ Give each child their name in large, cut-out paper letters for them to decorate.

Once children are starting to write their names, provide lots of opportunity for them to use their new skill:

■ Remind children to write their names on paintings and other work.

■ Put up large lists for children to sign. For example: *Who has used the computer today?* Attach your list to a board and provide a writing implement.

■ Take every possible opportunity to write names in greetings cards.

■ Ask children to write their names on decorated card discs. Laminate the discs and hang them on ribbons to make 'name necklaces'.

■ Ask children to write their names on a paper plate for snack time or lunch.

★ TIPS

Ask parents whose home language uses a different script to help you prepare a name card for their child to use alongside their English name card.

✓ READINESS

Children can be introduced to their name cards as soon as they arrive in the setting. If writing names does not happen spontaneously, introduce the activity once they have started to write letters on a blackboard or paper.

CURRICULUM GUIDANCE

Green stepping stone: *use writing as a means of recording and communicating*
ELG: *write their own names ...*
NLS/TEXT: *through guided and independent writing: write their own names*

Writing words

The following activities introduce the process of building and, later, writing simple CVC words. For other activities that can be used to encourage children to write words, see Chapter 5 (**Becoming a Reader**): *The reading basket* (pages 78–80), *High frequency word activities* (pages 80–1) and *Word games* (pages 81–3).

The word basket

This is a word-building activity that uses familiar objects with CVC names as its starting point. The activity involves segmenting a word into its separate sounds, choosing letters to represent those sounds and placing them in their correct order. For settings who are following the DfES (2004) '*Playing with Sounds*' approach, choose words/objects/pictures to fit in with the phoneme/grapheme correspondence groups (see **How to Use this Book**, pages 4–5).

Please note: this activity is closely linked with the activities in the **Segmenting words** section of Chapter 2 (pages 33–6).

Resources

- ✓ A set of cut-out letters
- ✓ A basket of familiar objects with CVC names, such as *dog*, *hat*, *pen*
- ✓ A mat (or magnetic board if you are using magnetic letters).

The activity

- ■ Sort out the letters that are needed to write the names of the objects, to limit the number of letters the child has to choose from.

- ■ Ask a child to select one of the objects, for example the cat.

- ■ Ask the children to help you segment the sounds that make up the word – *c-a-t*.

- ■ Ask a child to find the cut-out letter that represents the initial sound *c* and place it on the mat.

- ■ Continue for the middle and end sounds, *a* and *t*.

■ Point to each letter, say its sound and then repeat the word.

■ Ask a child to place the object beside the word.

■ Let the children continue with the activity using different objects.

★ TIPS

Emphasize placing the letters, side by side and in a straight line.

As children become ready, encourage them to try writing the words on a blackboard or paper.

Word chains

This activity shows children that substituting one grapheme for another can result in a different word.

Gather together a chain of familiar CVC objects with just one letter difference. For example:

pip / pup / cup / cap / cat / cot
bat / mat / man / fan / can / cap

You will need the same number of children as letters in the word chain (a group of eight for the above examples). Ask the children to help you make large letter necklaces representing each letter in the word chain. Put the items in a box and write out a list of the objects (in the correct order) to act as a prompt.

■ Give each child a letter necklace to wear.

■ Pick out the first item, ask the children to name it, and write its name on a whiteboard.

■ Ask the children to segment the word into its three sounds.

■ Help the children wearing the three corresponding letters to stand in a row, in the right order to spell the word.

■ Ask the rest of the group to check that they are spelling the word correctly by articulating each sound and then blending the sounds to read the word.

■ Place the item on a floor mat.

■ Pick out the next item, write its name under the first word and ask the children to identify which letter needs to change.

■ Help the children to switch places, in order to spell the new word.

■ Place the second item beneath the first.

■ Continue until all the items have been spelt and placed in a chain.

⭐ TIPS

Encourage the children to write the chain of words. Can they remember the order or do they need to refer to the row of items on the mat?

✓ READINESS

Before using **The word basket**, children need to have had some experience of segmenting words into their separate sounds (see **Segmenting words with 'I spy'**, page 34). They also need to know the sound/letter correspondences for the object names you have chosen (see **Textured letters**, pages 38–40). If you make cut-out letters and writing materials freely available, word building and writing words will often happen spontaneously. Before playing **Word chains** children should have had plenty of experience of word-building activities such as **The word basket**.

CURRICULUM GUIDANCE

Green stepping stone: *use writing as a means of recording and communicating*

ELG: *use their phonic knowledge to write simple regular words and make phonetically plausible attempts at more complex words*

NLS/TEXT: *through shared writing: apply knowledge of letter/sound correspondences in helping the teacher to scribe …*

Supported writing

The **Supported writing** activities enable any age group to record their thoughts, ideas and messages. **Dictation** is a one-to-one activity that can be used with even the youngest children. It helps to demonstrate the purpose and possibilities of writing, as well as allowing you to model the act of writing. **Shared writing** is a group activity for older children. It involves more input from the children over content, sentence construction and spelling words.

Dictation

Decide on the purpose of your written communication (see **Opportunities to write,** pages 68–71 for suggestions). Seat the child beside you and encourage him or her to talk about the chosen topic. Keep on highlighting the purpose of the writing. For example, if you are composing an invitation to a school picnic, help the child to include details such as where the picnic will take place. As you scribe the children's words, make sure that they can see what you are doing. Once you have finished, read through what you have written and check that the child is happy with the end result. Encourage the child to make changes – drafting and editing is an important element of becoming a whole writer.

⭐ TIPS

Your original copy may be a little rough! Explain to the child that you are going to '*write it out again neatly*'. Show the child the finished copy and compare with the original draft. For children with speech and communication difficulties, base the writing on a familiar object or picture.

Shared writing

Work on a large whiteboard or flip chart. Talk to the children about the purpose and subject matter of the writing and ask them to help you decide what to write. The following list covers just some of the elements that make up the act of writing as a whole. Introduce each aspect gradually, as children become ready:

- Talk about your title, its wording and where to position it on the page. How could you make the title stand out (using a different coloured pen, underlining)? Sometimes it is better to think about the title once the writing is complete.

- Show the children how to position the lines of writing on the page. This will vary, depending on whether you are writing prose, poetry, a list or some other writing format. As the children gain experience, ask them to tell you where to place the next word or sentence.

- Emphasize the gap between the words. When you have written a sentence, count through the words to help the children realize that a stream of speech is made up of separate words.

- Encourage the children to construct sentences that read well. Read back what you have written and ask the group to decide whether it sounds 'right'. Make changes if the group thinks it necessary.

- From time to time, ask the children to help you segment words into sounds: '*What sound does 'piglet' begin with?*' – and so on.

- Direct the children towards your **High frequency word bank** (see page 80) if they need help with spelling such words.

- Focus on ending sentences with a full stop and highlight when to use a capital letter.

⭐ TIPS

Give children individual whiteboards so that they can write simple words for themselves.

As a 'spin off' from looking at the organization of writing on the page, explore written languages with different layouts (such as Chinese or Arabic). Ask someone with knowledge of the language to help you prepare the activity.

✓ **READINESS**

Adapt **Dictation** to any age group or ability level by giving more or less support and choosing appropriate topics. Younger children need object-based subject matter, such as talking about a favourite toy. They may also need more prompting and their words will initially have to be 'embedded' in a sentence of your own making. To participate fully in **Shared writing**, children need a basic understanding of the purpose of writing. They should also be starting to segment words and be able to link some phonemes and graphemes.

CURRICULUM GUIDANCE

Green stepping stone: *begin to break the flow of speech into words*

Green stepping stone: *use writing as a means of recording and communicating*

ELG: *use their phonic knowledge to write simple regular words and make phonetically plausible attempts at more complex words*

ELG: *attempt writing for different purposes, using features of different forms such as lists, stories and instructions*

ELG: *... begin to form simple sentences, sometimes using punctuation*

NLS/TEXT: *through shared writing: understand that writing can be used for a range of purposes; understand that writing is formed directionally, a word at a time; apply knowledge of letter/sound correspondences in helping the teacher to scribe*

NLS/TEXT: *think about and discuss what they intend to write, ahead of writing it*

Independent writing

Independent writing can range from making 'writing-like' marks to extensive writing on chalkboards, whiteboards and paper. All literacy activities will support the child's development as an independent writer. Encourage children to write for themselves during free play (see Chapter 1, **Organizing the setting** section) and leave them to enjoy writing in their own way. Once children are starting to write more extensively, you can help them to focus on format and develop their skills of word building and sentence construction.

✓ **READINESS**

Children of all ages should be given the opportunity to write independently, at whatever stage of writing development they have reached.

Opportunities to write

Children learn best when encouraged to write in meaningful situations. The following suggestions are just a few of the many writing opportunities to be found in the early years setting.

CURRICULUM GUIDANCE

Blue stepping stone (writing): *ascribe meaning to marks*

Green stepping stone: *use writing as a means of recording and communicating*

ELG: *attempt writing for different purposes, using features of different forms such as lists, stories and instructions*

ELG: *... begin to form simple sentences, sometimes using punctuation*

NLS/TEXT: *through guided and independent writing: experiment with writing in a variety of play, exploratory and role-play situations*

Notes and messages

Ask the children to help you compose a note to be sent home. The note could be about a forthcoming trip, asking for items to be brought into school or inviting parents to come to an open day. Emphasize that the note is sending a message, telling carers what they need to know about the trip/project/visit. Make copies of **Photocopiable Writing Framework 1 ('a note from ...')**. Store them in the writing area so that children can send messages to others in the setting.

Writing about pictures

Choose a picture linked to a particular topic and scribe the children's responses. You can also write down the children's thoughts about their own paintings and drawings. This can be very useful for helping children (and parents) realize that their picture has meaning. It also makes the writing activity personal to the children – *their* painting, *their* thoughts and ideas.

 TIPS

When scribing the children's responses to their own paintings and drawings, discuss whether they are happy for you to write directly onto their picture or whether they would prefer you to write on the back or use a separate sheet of paper.

Calendars and diaries

Make a large laminated class calendar. Divide into seven sections and write the days of the week at the top of each section. Encourage the children to draw and write about their doings, to Blu-tak to the appropriate day. Keep a diary and ask the children to help you fill it in with special events such as birthdays.

Writing notices and signs

Writing is a significant way of passing on the kind of information that helps any community to run smoothly. Get the children to help you compose and write notices and signs. For example, *'please wash your hands'* in the toilets; *'this way to the garden'* on the patio door. Encourage the children to decide when and where a notice is needed. Use different shaped paper for writing the notices – a large arrow shape for *'this way to ...'* or a speech bubble for an informative notice (see **Photocopiable Writing Framework 3**).

Lists

A list is a very useful writing format. Make lists with the children whenever possible – lists of books; lists of writing materials in the writing area; lists of favourite animals/activities/songs/foods. Look out for independent list-making opportunities. For example, if a child tells you that a toy is broken, ask a small group to go round the setting, listing any items that need mending/replacing/cleaning. Use long, thin strips of paper to help the children learn how to set out a list. Make copies of **Photocopiable Writing Framework 1 ('my list')** and store in the writing area so that children can write their own lists.

Labels and captions

With the children, try labelling a picture of something with lots of parts – the body, a flower, an item of clothing. Add labels to a map of the setting or garden. Take a small group on a tour of the setting and find objects that need written labels. Writing captions for pictures is another useful way of exploring a theme or topic. Encourage the children to decide which aspect of the picture should be mentioned in the caption and show them how to attach the caption to the bottom of the picture. If writing captions for a series of pictures, check that they make sense as a sequence.

The computer

Introduce a simple word-processing program. Put stickers with lower case letters over the keyboard. As children become more adept with the computer, show them how to change the font style or the size of the print.

 TIPS

The computer can be useful for children who are struggling to form letters with a writing implement. As long as they can make attempts at building words, the computer will enable them to record their thoughts and messages in writing.

Non-written forms of recording

Encourage children to record their activities, thoughts, ideas and messages through drawing and painting, photographing, tape recording and videoing. These non-written forms of communication enable children to make their own records, long before they are able to write independently.

✓ READINESS

Opportunities to write can be adapted to any age group. Involve younger ones in mark-making, videoing, photographing and tape-recording activities. As children's understanding of the writing process develops, involve them in more complex activities such as writing captions or notices.

CURRICULUM GUIDANCE

Blue stepping stone: *ascribe meanings to marks*

Green stepping stone: *use writing as a means of recording and communicating*

ELG: *attempt writing for different purposes, using features of different forms such as lists, stories and instructions*

ELG: *write their own names and other things such as labels and captions, and begin to form simple sentences, sometimes using punctuation*

NLS/TEXT: *through shared writing: understand that writing can be used for a range of purposes, e.g. to send messages, record, inform, tell stories*

NLS/TEXT: *through guided and independent writing: experiment with writing in a variety of play, exploratory and role-play situations; write labels and captions for pictures and drawings; write sentences to match pictures or sequences of drawings*

Useful Resources

Lower Case Lacing Letters (ref. E51691)
26 plastic letters with holes for lacing.
Small Creative Sand Tray (ref. G15614)
For writing in sand; includes smoothing tool.
Available from: NES Arnold

Letter Shapes (ref.1392)
8 printed wooden boards with writing related patterns such as loops and zig-zags.
Available from: WESCO

Literacy Dry Wipe Boards (ref. 010277)
Pack of 30 A4 boards with guidelines on one side, blank on reverse.
Slate Chalk Boards (ref. 006366)
Pack of 5.
Busybase Mobile Easel (ref. MPEE 1051)
Easel on casters, adjustable height, whiteboard surface and clamp for flip chart.
Available from: The Consortium

Reading Rods (DEP12023/DEP 12024/DEP 12025)
3 sets of interlocking bricks with consonants, short and long vowels, and letter blends for word building and exploring word families.
Available from: Education Supplies Directory

Literacy Role Play Props: Red Post Box (ref. E26269)
Post Office (ref. G12091)
Self-contained play centre.
Available from: NES Arnold

See **Useful Addresses,** pages 126–7, for suppliers' contact details.

Photocopiable Writing Framework 1 (list/note)

a note from

my list

Photocopiable Writing Framework 2 (recipe)

RECIPE
FOR

_____

ingredients

method

Name _____

Photocopiable Writing Framework 3
(postcard/speech bubble)

Becoming a Reader

In this chapter ...
This chapter focuses on the many different elements that come together to make up the act of reading. The chapter is divided into three sections: ■ Reading in the environment ■ Reading activities: words ■ Reading activities: phrases and sentences.

Reading in the environment

We live in a print-rich environment and it is important that this is replicated in the setting. For more ideas on how to inspire children to read within the setting see Chapter 1 (**The Setting**).

Print all around us!

The following activities focus on exploring environmental print. Signs, notices and labels are everywhere, while boxes, bags and food containers provide endless reading opportunities.

Reading notices and signs

Encourage the children to have a go at reading signs and notices within the setting and beyond. Take a small group on a tour of the setting and find lots of different environmental print to read. Involve the children in making a large map of the setting and ask them to help you write out some of the shorter notices and signs to stick on the map. Give them word, phrase or sentence cards and ask them to find the matching sign or notice in the setting; for example, *Ladies / Fire Exit / Please wash your hands*. Use photos of the signs to make a display chart.

⭐ **TIPS**

Link this activity with ***Writing notices and signs*** (page 70).

Looking for signs and notices around the setting can be useful for children who find it hard to sit still. Keep children with a short attention span on task by challenging them to spot a sign on the toilet door and so on.

A wrappings chart

Encourage children to explore food labels, bags and wrappings by displaying them as a wall chart. If children bring in a packed lunch or snack, look out for common containers. If particular shops dominate your area, include their carrier bags in your display. Send home a note asking parents to save wrappings from commonly used foods. Ask the children to help you stick the wrappings onto a large sheet of card. Talk about the wrappings as you work – which do the children recognize, can they read any of the words? Decide on a heading for the chart, for example: *Which is your favourite food?* Display the chart alongside a box of matching wrappings. Encourage the children to match wrappings from the box with the wrappings on the chart. If children bring in foods from home, can they find the wrapping on the chart?

⭐ **TIPS**

Ask parents from different ethnic and cultural backgrounds to supply you with appropriate wrappings for the chart.

✓ **READINESS**

Introduce ***Reading notices and signs*** once children have started to recognize letters and some familiar and common words. Encourage younger children and those who are not yet reading to match food wrappings by colour and design. Once children are starting to read words, they can be helped to read some of the print.

CURRICULUM GUIDANCE

Yellow stepping stone: *show interest in ... print in the environment*

Blue stepping stone: *know information can be relayed in the form of print*

Green stepping stone: *begin to recognise some familiar words*

ELG: *read a range of familiar and common words and simple sentences independently*

NLS/TEXT: *to recognise printed ... words in a variety of settings*

Word displays

Choose an area of the environment, such as the sand box. Ask the children to help you think of words linked with sand and sand play. For example, *bucket, sieve, sandy, grainy, yellow*, *brown*. Ask the children to help you write the words on cards. Choose some interesting ways of decorating the words. Glue sand around *sandy*; write *bucket* onto a card cut into the shape of a bucket; stick a variety of rough textures onto the cut-out letters for the word *grainy*. Encourage the children to come up with their own ideas for decorating the words. Display the words near the area and help the children to read them. Keep adding new words to the display. Think of some different ways to display the words – for example, hang them from a wire coat hanger to make a mobile.

⭐ **TIPS**

Encourage the children to choose their own areas of the setting as the basis for a word display, and think of the words they would like to include.

✓ **READINESS**

Children of all ages can explore words related to a topic, and join in the art element of this activity. To gain fully from the reading/writing part of the activity, children need to have grasped the concept of words and understand that print holds meaning.

CURRICULUM GUIDANCE

Yellow stepping stone: *show interest in ... print in the environment*

Blue stepping stone: *know information can be relayed in the form of print*

Green stepping stone: *begin to recognise some familiar words*

ELG: *read a range of familiar and common words and simple sentences independently*

NLS/WORD: *make collections of ... words linked to particular topics*

NLS/TEXT: *to recognise printed ... words in a variety of settings*

Reading activities: words

Preparation for reading begins with sharing picture books, enjoying rhymes and rhythms, exploring the sounds of language and learning to link letters and sounds. The next stage is for the child to use phonic knowledge and sight recognition to start reading simple and familiar words.

Although the children can be helped to read the words, it is important that they feel successful as independent readers. As much as possible, adapt the difficulty of the words to match the level of your young readers.

For settings who are following the *DfES* (2004) *Playing with Sounds* approach, choose words to fit in with the phoneme/grapheme correspondence groups (see **How to Use this Book**, pages 4–5).

The reading basket

This activity is a first introduction to reading simple CVC words. The children are shown how to identify the letter/sound correspondences in a written word and blend the sounds to read the whole word.

Resources

✓   A basket containing a collection of objects with CVC names, such as:

pig hen dog bed cat ted pen mug
bag peg rat bun rug jug bat

If you have children in the group with CVC names, such as *Tim* or *Sam*, add their photos to the basket.

✓   Word cards with the names of the items

✓   Strips of paper and a pencil.

The activity

■   Introduce some of the objects to a small group of children.
■   Let the children explore the objects and check that they are using the same name as the word card (for example, *hen* rather than *chicken*).
■   Ask a child to choose one of the objects, for example the *pig*.
■   Introduce the corresponding word card and explain that you are going to read the word.
■   Point to each letter in turn and encourage the children to help you articulate each sound.
■   Blend the sounds to read the whole word – *pig*.
■   Put the word card next to the pig.
■   Gradually draw the children into articulating and blending the sounds for themselves.
■   As children become able to read CVC words without the context of the object, give them a word card and ask them to find the object in the basket.

⭐ TIPS

Highlight the link between reading and writing by writing the names of the objects on strips of paper for the children to read. Encourage them to write the words for themselves.

Once older/able children become more confident with CVC words, introduce some common digraphs such as *ch*, *sh*, *th*, *ll*, *ng* and *ck*. Encourage the children to tackle some longer, regular words as they come across them in books and other print forms – for example, *brush*, *robin*, *singing*, *chicken*, *umbrella*.

✓ READINESS

This activity can be introduced once children have had some experience with sound/letter correspondences. Some children take a long time to grasp the process of sounding out and blending sounds. As long as the child is enjoying the activity, keep persevering. Make it fun, use lots of different objects and choose items that hold a particular interest for the child. Remember also that some children respond much better to sight recognition of words.

High frequency word activities

The following activities focus on the *National Literacy Strategy Framework's* list of high frequency words for Reception (DfEE, 1998). These are the words that children need to know, in order to tackle even the simplest of texts. Many of them cannot be sounded out and have to be sight learnt. For a full list of the words, see **Photocopiable Sheet 3: Phonics/High Frequency Word Record** (Chapter 7).

A high frequency word bank

Store the high frequency word cards in a word bank. This makes the cards easily accessible and enables you to have the words on permanent display. Construct some sturdy card or fabric charts with pockets for holding the cards. Velcro or glue the words to the front of each pocket and store several laminated word cards in the appropriate pockets.

⭐ TIPS

Display strips of paper/pencils nearby and encourage children to write the words for themselves.

Exploring high frequency words in big books

Matching words: choose one or two high frequency words to look out for during a big book ***Shared reading*** session (see pages 88–90). Ask children to match high frequency word cards with words in the text.

Cloze: once children know a story well, cover all the examples of a high frequency word with labels. As you read through the story, ask the children to supply the missing words and then peel off the labels to check if they were right.

Exploring high frequency word shapes

Find lots of different ways to explore the shapes and spellings of the words. Count the letters in the words and sort into one, two, three and four letter groups. Sort words according to their initial sounds/letters. Sort out the words that end with *e* – do they all rhyme? Which is the longest word? Which are the shortest words? Which words begin and end with the same letter?

Sorting high frequency words

Look out for examples of high frequency words in magazines, leaflets and other printed literature. Give each child a word card and ask them to search for that word in the text. Help them to cut out the samples and put them into the correct pocket in the ***High frequency word bank***.

⭐ TIPS

Give the children single pages or small chunks of text to look through. Include text with samples of the words in large-print titles.

✓ READINESS

Children should already have been exposed to high frequency words through looking at the text of picture books and other printed literature. Introduce two or three words at a time, once children can link sounds and letters and are starting to read CVC words. Start off with simple words that can be sounded out (*dog, am, man*). As soon as possible, introduce the most common phonetically irregular words such as *the, you* and *I*.

CURRICULUM GUIDANCE

Blue stepping stones: *know information can be relayed in the form of print and under-stand the concept of a word*

Green stepping stone: *begin to recognise some familiar words*

ELG: *read a range of familiar and common words and single sentences independently*

NLS/WORD: *read on sight a range of familiar words; read on sight the 45 high frequency words to be taught by the end of YR*

Word games

The following activities are all based on reading and acting upon single words. The link between reading and writing can be highlighted by encouraging children to write the words, once they have played the various reading games.

The 'I can' game

Prepare a set of action word cards, for example *hop, run, jog, tap, pat, skip, jump, sing, brush, kick,* plus the high frequency words, *see, look* and *go*. Ask a child to read a card and then perform the action, using props where appropriate (a ball to *kick*, a drum to *tap*). Write an action word for a child to read in secret, then put out two or three action cards and ask the group to guess which of the actions the child is performing.

⭐ **TIPS**

This activity can be useful for children who have difficulty following instructions. If they can perform the action, you will know that they have understood what is required of them.

If you need to give certain children additional support, provide photographs alongside the word cards. Take photos of children performing obvious actions with a prop (*patting* a toy dog, *jumping* over a puddle).

Children who are struggling with the **Reading basket** sometimes find it easier to read the CVC action words (*hop*, *tap*, *run*).

Labelling the setting

Prepare a set of word cards with names of objects in the setting, for example *mat*, *cup*, *peg*, *book*, *pencil*, *snack table*. Ask each child in the group to read an object word card, find the object in the setting and place the word card beside it, to act as a label.

⭐ **TIPS**

If necessary, provide photos of the objects along with the word cards.

Animal words

Prepare a set of animal word cards, for example *cat* and *dog* (high frequency words), *pig*, *hen*, *ant*, *chick*, *cow*, *bee*, *spider*. Ask a child to read a card and then role play the animal. As with the action cards, you can ask the group to guess which animal the child is pretending to be.

⭐ **TIPS**

Ask an assistant to help model the role play/animal noises.

If necessary, provide pictures as well as word cards.

Go fish!

Gather together a collection of waterproof items with CVC names, for example a *dog*, a *cat*, a *bug*, a *fish* (plastic models), a *cup*, a *zip*, a *pen*, a *tin*. Prepare a word card for each item, plus some cards with 'nonsense' words such as '*sen*' and '*fno*'. Place the items in the water-play tank. Give each child a net and a word card to read. Once they have read their word, instruct them to 'go fish' for their item. When they have fished their item out of the water, ask them to check that it matches the word card before returning it to the water. Continue the process with a different word card. Make sure that you give the 'nonsense' cards to children who won't be fazed by not being able to recognize the word. Involve the whole group in deciding whether the word makes sense. Have fun with the children – urge them to go fish for a *fno* or a *sen*!

⭐ **TIPS**

If possible, choose items that float. Be ready to help a child fish out a small, non-floating item.

✓ **READINESS**

As soon as children can read simple words, you can introduce the CVC words for these games. For example, *mat*, *cup* (***Labelling the setting***). As children become ready, offer more demanding words such as *donkey* (***Animal words***) and *brush* (***The 'I can' game***).

CURRICULUM GUIDANCE

Blue stepping stone (reading): *understand the concept of a word*

Green stepping stone (reading): *begin to recognise some familiar words*

ELG (reading): *read a range of familiar and common words … independently*

ELG (linking sounds and letters): *hear and say initial and final sounds in words and short vowel sounds within words*

NLS/WORD: *read on sight a range of familiar words; read on sight the 45 high frequency words to be taught by the end of YR*

A *reading flap book*

Use familiar CVC words as the basis for making your own flap book. This helps the children to discover that the same words crop up time and again, as well as encouraging them to practise their word reading skills.

Resources

✓ A large, unlined scrap book with sturdy pages

✓ Thin card, scissors and strong tape (for making the flaps)

✓ Photos of familiar CVC objects

✓ Felt pens/pencils.

Making the book

Ask the children to help you choose and photograph objects for the book. Stick a photo on each page of the scrap book. Explore the construction of simple flap books such as Rod Campbell's *Dear Zoo* (Puffin). Write each object's name on a square of card and tape the cards over the corresponding pictures to make movable flaps. Involve the children in making the cover for the book and planning a title – for example, *What's Under the Flap?*

⭐ TIPS

Helping to take photos can enable children who find it difficult to sit still to engage in this activity.

Planning and constructing your own book provides a useful 'way in' for children who are not showing much interest in books.

✓ READINESS

All children can help to choose objects and take photos for the book. To be involved fully, children need to be confident with reading and writing CVC words.

CURRICULUM GUIDANCE

Blue stepping stone: *understand the concept of a word*

Green stepping stone: *begin to recognise some familiar words*

ELG: *read a range of familiar and common words … independently*

ELG: *explore and experiment with sounds, words and texts*

NLS/WORD: *read on sight a range of familiar words*

NLS/TEXT: *understand and use correctly terms about books and print: book, cover … page, word, letter, title*

NLS/TEXT: *distinguish between writing and drawing in books and in own work*

Rime sorting boxes

This activity encourages the children to focus on the spelling of rimes in simple CVC words.

Resources

- ✓ A basket containing small groups of objects/pictures with rhyming CVC names:

  cat / hat / bat
  pen / hen / Ben
  top / shop / mop

- ✓ A word card for each object

- ✓ Small post boxes or tins with a rime (for example, *-op*) written on the lid.

The activity

- ■ Choose two or three rime groups.

- ■ Let the children explore the items and check that they are using the same names as those on the word cards.

■ Introduce the word cards and ask the children to match the word cards and items, as in *The reading basket*.

■ If the children have not already noticed, point out that the words make rhyming groups.

■ Look at the word cards and identify the rimes.

■ Ask the children to match each rime with a rime on the post box and post the cards into the correct box.

■ When all the cards have been posted, open up the boxes and check that each group of word cards has the same rime.

■ As children become more adept at the activity, introduce more rime groups to sort and encourage them to work without the context of the objects.

✓ READINESS
Introduce this activity once children have had some experience with the process of blending separate phonemes to read a word (as in *The reading basket*).

CURRICULUM GUIDANCE

Blue stepping stone (reading): *understand the concept of a word*

Green stepping stone (reading): *begin to recognise some familiar words*

ELG (reading): *read a range of familiar and common words ... independently*

ELG (linking sounds and letters): *hear and say initial and final sounds in words and short vowel sounds within words*

NLS/WORD: *reading letter(s) that represent the sound(s): a–z, ch, sh, th*

NLS/WORD: *using knowledge of rhyme to identify families of rhyming CVC words; discriminating onsets from rimes in speech and spelling*

Reading activities: phrases and sentences

Individual words are just the building blocks of a text. As soon as possible, encourage the children to read and interpret phrases and sentences, including shared reading sessions where you can model the process of reading a whole text.

Phrase and sentence games
Treasure hunt

Write out some simple instructions using action words and the names of objects or areas of the setting. For example, *hop to the mats*; *jog to the milk jug*; *run to the snack table*;

look in the book corner; *look on Sam's peg*; *go to the red pencil tin*. When you have written out the sentences, keep one as the first clue and hide the rest in the relevant places. For example, if clue number 1 reads '*go to the mats*' you will need to hide clue number 2 among the mats. Help a small group of children to read the first clue and explain that when they arrive at the mats, they must search for the next clue. The final clue should lead to the treasure. Hide some chocolate coins or pendants made from gold card for your treasure hunters to find.

⭐ TIPS

You may need eyes in the back of your head to ensure that other children don't move the clues before the treasure hunters find them.

The active nature of this game can be useful for children who have difficulty sitting still; ask an assistant to keep the child on task, if necessary.

On the chair

Make a set of word cards with different position words, for example *on*, *in*, *under*, *beside*, *behind*, *inside*, *up*, *near*, *below*. Choose two items such as a teddy and a chair or a toy car and a model bridge. Write out word cards for your two items – *the teddy* and *the chair*. You will also need a card for the word *put*.

- Introduce the items and word cards to a small group of children.

- Arrange the word cards to make an instruction – *put the teddy **on** the chair*.

- Help the children to read the sentence and ask a child to carry out the instruction.

- Change the position word – *put the teddy **behind** the chair*.

- Help the children to read the new sentence and ask a child to move the teddy to the appropriate position.

- As the children become familiar with the words, encourage them to play the game independently and write their own sentences.

⭐ TIPS

Have fun with word combinations such as *put the chair on the teddy*.

If a sentence can't be acted out, such as *put the teddy inside the chair*, encourage the children to find something that teddy can be put inside, such as *the box*.

What kind?

This activity introduces different describing words (adjectives). It helps children to discover that certain words tell you *about* something.

- Choose pairs of objects with different features or make some simple drawings – for example, a *big dog* and a *small dog*, a *sad man* and a *happy man*, a *red cup* and a *green cup*, a *round biscuit* and a *square biscuit*, a *long pen* and a *short pen*.

- Make separate word cards for each object and adjective: *red* / *green* / *cup* / *big* / *small* / *dog* and so on. You will also need several word cards for *the*.

- Arrange the word cards to make a phrase, for example *the dog*.

- Help the children to read the phrase and ask them to place 'the dog' beside the phrase.

- Whether they choose the *big* or the *small* dog, point out that they can't be sure which of the two dogs to choose.

- Put an adjective – *big* – between *the* and *dog*.

- Read the phrase, and emphasize that now the children know which dog to choose.

- Continue with other phrases and objects/pictures.

✓ READINESS
Introduce these activities once children are coping with CVC words and the most common high frequency words such as *the*, *is* and *to*. Help the children to read the words they don't know and remind them of any high frequency words they may have forgotten.

CURRICULUM GUIDANCE

Blue stepping stone: *know information can be relayed in the form of print*
ELG: *read a range of familiar and common words and simple sentences independently*
NLS/WORD: *read on sight a range of familiar words; read on sight the 45 high frequency words to be taught by the end of YR; to read on sight the words from texts of appropriate difficulty*

High frequency word sentences
Jumbled sentences

Look in a favourite book to find a simple sentence containing the high frequency word you wish to focus on. Write out the sentence, highlighting the word in a different colour, and cut it into separate words/phrases. Ask the children to put the words in the right order and check against the sentence in the book.

A high frequency word display

Choose a simple phrase or sentence containing one or more high frequency words. For example: ***I am*** Mrs Perkins. / ***We play in the*** sand pit. / ***The*** red **cat**. Write the words in large letters, highlighting the high frequency words with a different colour. Ask the children to make paintings to illustrate the phrases or sentences. Stick the words and pictures to large sheets of card and display in the setting. As the children come across more words, encourage them to write and illustrate further sentences to add to the chart.

⭐ TIPS

Make the words in the display the same size as your high frequency word cards. Challenge the children to match a word card with a word in the display and Blu-tak the word card on top.

Hunt the high frequency word!

Hide simple sentence or phrase cards containing high frequency words. Give each child a different word card and ask them to hunt for a sentence containing their word. Give them clues – '*you will find a sentence card with your word in the home corner*'. Once children have found their sentence or phrase, help them to read it.

⭐ TIPS

As most of the sentence and phrase cards will contain more than one high frequency word, make sure you hide lots of samples.

Unless you have a good memory, make a list of where you have hidden each card.

The active nature of this activity can be useful for children who have difficulty sitting still; ask an assistant to help the child keep on task, if necessary.

✓ READINESS

Use these activities to reinforce the high frequency words with children who are starting to read phrases and sentences.

CURRICULUM GUIDANCE

Blue stepping stones: *know information can be relayed in the form of print and understand the concept of a word*

Green stepping stone: *begin to recognise some familiar words*

ELG: *read a range of familiar and common words and single sentences independently*

NLS/WORD: *read on sight a range of familiar words; read on sight the 45 high frequency words to be taught by the end of YR*

Shared reading

Start off by choosing a big book version of a picture book for your shared reading session. Have just one or two main aims per session and repeat a book several times so that the children can gradually build up their understanding of the story. The following list covers just some of the many literacy elements and skills you can introduce:

- Look at the cover of the book and read the title. Talk about how it stands out – the size of the letters, the colour of the print, its position on the cover. Look at the pictures on the front and back covers. What do the children think the story might be about?

- For the first session, read at a normal pace. As the children get to know the story, encourage them to join in with rhyming words and repeated refrains.

- Use the pictures to help the children predict, interpret and make sense of the story.

- From time to time, point to the individual words as you read and highlight the left to right direction of the text.

- Emphasize the move from the end of one line to the start of the next. Explore the appearance of different layouts, such as poetry, dialogue, paragraphs, speech bubbles and different-sized scripts.

- From time to time, encourage children to read any words they might recognize. Apart from sight recognition, get them using their phonics skills to help you read simple words.

- Help the children to use picture clues and the context of the story to read new words. Try the cloze technique, where you leave out a tricky word and then go back to see what might fit into the sentence.

- Use the text to focus on elements such as rhyming words, specific high frequency words, a particular letter/sound link, digraphs and consonant clusters, capital letters and full stops.

⭐ TIPS

Use a pointer rather than your finger so that your hand does not obscure the text.

Put out some standard size copies of the book in the book corner, for independent reading.

Ensure that your book choices offer positive models of race, gender and disability.

✓ READINESS

One of the many advantages of shared reading is that each child can participate at their own level. As a starting point, have a core group of children who can make attempts at reading words using sight recognition and phonics knowledge. These children will help to model early reading strategies for the rest of the group.

CURRICULUM GUIDANCE

Blue stepping stone: *know information can be relayed in the form of print*

ELG: *read a range of familiar and common words and simple sentences independently*

NLS/WORD: *read on sight a range of familiar words; read on sight the 45 high frequency words to be taught by the end of YR; read on sight the words from texts of appropriate difficulty*

NLS/TEXT: *to understand and use correctly terms about books and print: book, cover, beginning, end, page, line, word, letter, title; to track the text in the right order, page by page, left to right, top to bottom; to distinguish between writing and drawing in books …*

NLS/TEXT: *to use a variety of cues when reading: knowledge of the story and its context, and awareness of how it should make sense grammatically; to re-read a text to provide context cues to help read unfamiliar words; to understand how story book language works …; to re-read frequently a variety of familiar texts, e.g. big books …; to locate and read significant parts of the text, e.g. picture captions, names of key characters, rhymes and chants … speech bubbles, italicized, enlarged words*

NLS/SENTENCE: *to use awareness of the grammar of a sentence to predict words during shared reading and when re-reading familiar stories; that words are ordered left to right and need to be read that way to make sense*

Useful Resources

Sentence Strips (ref. 010838)
Blank coloured strips for writing phrase/sentence reading material.
Standard Pocket Chart (ref. 010987)
Chart with clear pockets for displaying words/sentences.
Available from: The Consortium

Easy Words to Sound Bingo (ref. E58430)
Bingo game based on CVC and simple words.
Simple Sentence Snap (ref. E58429)
Snap game using simple sentences.
Available from: NES Arnold

Blank Word Washing Line (ref. G23519)
Line, pegs and wipe clean cards for creating word families, sentences, etc.
Available from: NES Arnold

First Words Pack
36 A4 colour posters showing words or phrases for sight recognition. Includes nouns, adjectives, verbs and some high frequency words.
Available from: Practical Pre-school

See **Useful Addresses**, pages 126–7, for suppliers' contact details.

The Role of the Picture Book

In this chapter ...

The picture book is central to the development of literacy. This chapter explores the many different aspects of books and story, and how they can help the child to become a fully literate individual. The chapter is divided into three sections:

- ■ Sharing picture books

- ■ Exploring picture books

- ■ Story structure.

Sharing picture books

Sharing picture books with an adult is perhaps the single most important activity when it comes to literacy development. One-to-one, small story groups, large story groups and independent reading should be a major part of every child's day.

Story groups

Story groups offer a welcome opportunity for children to settle down and simply enjoy the story. Lots of learning will come naturally from the session, but the priority should always be the fun, pleasure and relaxation to be gained from books.

Individual and small story groups

Sharing a picture book with an individual or small group is hugely valuable, particularly if you allow the children to converse freely about the book. If timetabling one-to-one reading is difficult, try to keep your group to a minimum of three children.

As part of your individual/small group reading sessions, bear in mind the following:

■ Seat the children so that they are on either side of you; this enables them to see the print and the pictures as you read.

■ Give the children plenty of time to study the pictures. Only turn the page when their attention has shifted.

■ Encourage the children to talk about the book by responding positively and fully to any comments or questions. Include a talkative child in the group, to model book-based conversation for the rest.

■ Plan an open-ended stretch of time for the session. Once certain children realize that conversation is a part of book sharing, the session can last a very long time!

■ If you have to wind up the session before you have finished the book, paraphrase the pages and read the end of the story. This ensures that the children do not miss out on this important aspect of story structure.

■ Make a note of the books you have shared with each child and repeat favourites as often as possible. Encourage children to choose their own books for a story session.

■ As you repeat books, watch out for the same questions and topics of conversation emerging with each reading. Take the opportunity to build on the child's understanding of the story.

★ TIPS

Ask parent helpers, visitors and students to share books with individuals.

If you have children who find it difficult to sit still, introduce an active element to the story session. Use a book such as Eric Carle's *Head to Toe* (Puffin), where the child can join in the actions.

Make the most of one-to-one sessions to support children with communication difficulties. The shared focus of the book is often helpful when it comes to understanding children's speech.

Large story groups

Reading a story to a large group of children is a much more adult-led process than an individual or small group session. Bear in mind the following:

■ Make sure that all the children can see the pictures. Use a big book whenever possible.

■ Learn to read upside down so that you can hold the book open on your lap. Combine this with lots of small group sessions, so that the children can see you holding and reading the book in a 'normal' manner.

- You will usually have to work a little harder at holding the children's attention during a large group story. Try the following:

  - Always run through a story before you read it – the better you know the text, the more eye contact you can make with the children.

  - As you read the story, make good use of the 'pregnant pause' to build up suspense and focus attention on what might happen next.

  - Use facial expressions and special voices for different characters, although do bear in mind that some children can be disturbed to see their teacher suddenly turn into a tiger or an ogre!

  - If a child's attention wanders, draw him back into the story with a challenge – *'Tom, can you see the tiger in the picture?'*

- Use big group sessions to highlight social/emotional issues. For example, choose a story with a sharing theme and link the story with the children's own experiences.

- Although questions and comments have to be more limited than in a small group, encourage the children to share their emotional responses. Do the events of the story make them feel amused, sad, frightened?

⭐ TIPS

After a story session, put the book in the book corner and encourage the children to look at it independently.

✓ READINESS

Introduce story groups as soon as children arrive in your setting. Tailor your choice of reading to suit the child's age, ability level and interests. Younger children and children with limited experience of books can find a one-to-one or small group arrangement easier than a large group story session.

CURRICULUM GUIDANCE

Yellow stepping stones: *listen to and join in with stories and poems, one-to-one and also in small groups* and *show interest in illustrations and print in books …*

Blue stepping stones: *have favourite books; know information can be relayed in the form of print; hold books the correct way up and turn pages*

Green stepping stone: *enjoy an increasing range of books*

ELG: *know that print carries meaning …*

NLS/TEXT: *understand how story book language works…; re-read frequently a variety of familiar texts*

Using books independently

Exploring books independently is important to the children's developing sense of themselves as readers. Make your book corner as enticing as possible and display books throughout the setting. For suggestions on creating a book corner and encouraging the use of books through play, see Chapter 1 (**The Setting**).

⭐ TIPS

As soon as children arrive in your setting, introduce them to the book corner. Show them how to access and replace the books. Keep reiterating these practical skills and encourage the children to use the book corner appropriately.

✓ READINESS

Children of all ages should be encouraged to explore books independently.

CURRICULUM GUIDANCE

Blue stepping stones: *have favourite books; handle books carefully; know information can be relayed in the form of print; hold books the correct way up and turn pages*

Green stepping stone: *enjoy an increasing range of books*

ELG: *explore and experiment with sounds, words and texts*

ELG: *know that print carries meaning …*

NLS/TEXT: *re-read frequently a variety of familiar texts*

Exploring picture books

Getting to grips with the book as 'an object' is important if the children are to become familiar and comfortable with books. There are many activities that can encourage children to explore different kinds of books, as well as their physical aspects and how they are constructed.

Different types of books

Introduce children to the world of books by focusing on different formats, illustrations, themes and subject matter. Wherever possible, follow the children's lead. For example, if a book with textured pictures is exciting interest, introduce some more novelty books. The following are just some of the themes or formats that you can use as a starting point for your explorations:

Flap books: examine the different ways of constructing a flap book. Do the flaps open sideways (like a door) or upwards (like a trap door)? Is the flap cut into a particular shape, such as a bush with an animal hiding beneath? Look at how the flaps are attached to the page and discuss how they need to be handled carefully. Make a collection of flap books to display in the book corner. Construct your own flap book, using inspiration from the books in your collection. Involve the children in choosing a theme for the book, planning the size and shape of the flaps and exploring ways of attaching the flaps to the pages. See *A reading flap book* (pages 83–4) and *Making books* (pages 96–8) for further ideas.

Novelty books: stimulate the senses with textured books, scented books, books that make sounds when you open the page and books with added extras such as 'mirror' paper. Display the books and add labels explaining which 'sense' the book appeals to (a large picture of a nose beside the 'smelly' books is fun). Make your own 'senses' book. Look at how a texture has been incorporated into a picture, for example a dog with a 'real' fur tummy. Gather together different materials and encourage the children to come up with picture ideas to incorporate each material. Make 'smelly' pictures for the book using dried herbs and scraps of scented drawer lining paper.

Different sizes and formats: books come in all shapes and sizes: big books, miniature books, hardbacks, paperbacks, board books, fabric books. The best way to explore different formats is to choose a few books and collect as many versions as you can find. Classic picture books are often published in hardback, paperback, board, as a celebration edition and as a big book. Explore the different formats with the children and ask them to think about the purposes of each one. For example, when is it better to use a board book rather than a paperback? Display the different editions in the book corner.

Content: focusing on different categories of books helps young children to make sense of the huge choice available to them. As with novelty books, follow the children's interest. For example, if toy cars and lorries are popular in your setting, start a collection of books with a vehicle theme. If you are doing lots of work with rhythm and rhyme, gather together different rhyme collections and books with rhyming text. Some possible content themes include poetry, traditional rhymes and stories, colour, number, opposites, word books, abc's, information books and encyclopaedias.

Illustrations: illustrations are an important element of the picture book as a whole and there are many different illustrative styles to be explored. As a starting point, gather together some books with photographed illustrations and some with painted illustrations. Link the two different types of illustration to the children's own experiences of painting and taking photographs. Gradually introduce other categories such as collage pictures, cartoons and line drawings. Ask each child to choose their favourite picture and talk about why they like it. Use *Dictation* techniques (pages 66–7) to record their responses.

 TIPS
Exploring pictures can provide a useful way in for children who are not showing much enthusiasm for books.

✓ READINESS

Children of all ages can investigate different types of books. Tailor the activity to suit the age and ability level of the children: offer simple flap books to younger ones while encouraging older ones to explore the construction of more complex novelty books.

CURRICULUM GUIDANCE

Yellow stepping stone: *show interest in illustrations and print in books*

Blue stepping stones: *have favourite books; know information can be relayed in the form of print; hold books the correct way up and turn pages*

Green stepping stone: *enjoy an increasing range of books*

ELG: *explore and experiment with sounds, words and texts*

ELG: *know that print carries meaning …*

NLS / TEXT: *distinguish between writing and drawing in books …*

Making books

Making your own books is a great way to familiarize children with 'the book' as a physical object, as well as offering endless writing and storying possibilities.

Resources

✓ Plain paper and card

✓ Writing implements

✓ Darning needle and button thread/hole puncher and ribbon (for joining the pages).

Making the book

Naming the parts: start off by exploring and naming the physical aspects of the book – *cover, page, title*. Challenge older ones with some more unusual terms – *spine, gutter* (the trench between the left and right hand pages), *blurb* (the information on the back of the book), *ISBN* (the reference code on the back of the book).

Constructing the book: decide on the technique you want to use. There are three main possibilities:

1   Zig-zag book – fold a strip of paper into a concertina to create separate 'pages' (fig. 1).

2   Ribbon book – use a hole puncher to punch holes in the top left hand corner of the pages and tie them together with a ribbon (fig. 2).

3   Sewn book – fold rectangles of paper in half to create pages and sew them down the crease (fig. 3).

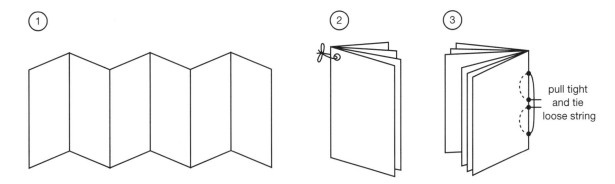

The content: there are endless possibilities regarding content. The book can be based on a particular theme or topic. Alternatively, it could be a group story book, either the retelling of an old favourite (see ***Recounting stories***, pages 103–4) or a story the class have made up, together. Other subject matter could include:

- group diary

- picture/word book

- collection of illustrated rhymes/songs

- catalogue of favourite activities/playground equipment/writing materials

- book reviews

- theme book (colours/opposites/shapes)

- alphabet book.

Designing the book: there are many design aspects that have to be considered – size, shape and colour of pages; the type of paper for the pages and cover; cover information such as title, authors, blurb; whether the pictures will be photos, paintings, drawings ... the list is endless! Encourage the children to look at lots of different books to get some ideas and give them a range of papers to choose from. Help them to think about their choices – is corrugated card suitable for the pages or would it be better for the cover? If they choose dark red pages, how can they make the writing show up?

★ TIPS

Planning and constructing your own book can provide a useful way in for children who are not showing much interest in books.

✓ READINESS

Children of all ages can contribute to making a group book. Ensure that older ones are fully involved in planning, constructing and writing the book. Younger ones can help with activities such as drawing, sticking and decorating the pages. All age groups should be encouraged to look at the finished book.

> ## CURRICULUM GUIDANCE
>
> **Yellow stepping stone:** *show interest in illustrations and print in books*
>
> **Blue stepping stones:** *have favourite books; know information can be relayed in the form of print; hold books the correct way up and turn pages*
>
> **Green stepping stone:** *enjoy an increasing range of books*
>
> **ELG:** *explore and experiment with sounds, words and texts*
>
> **ELG:** *know that print carries meaning …*
>
> **ELG:** *retell narratives in the correct sequence, drawing on language patterns of stories*
>
> **NLS/TEXT:** *distinguish between writing and drawing in books and in own work; use experience of stories, poems and simple recounts as a basis for independent writing*

The author and illustrator

Introduce children to the concept of 'the author' as the person who wrote the story, and 'the illustrator' as the person who created the pictures.

Introducing the author/illustrator: start off by choosing an author/illustrator whose work is familiar to the group. Find the name of the author on the front cover. Do the children know anyone else with the same first or family name? If possible, show the children a picture of the author (write to the publisher asking for information, prior to introducing this activity). Link the author's role with the children's own experience of telling stories and making books. Link the illustrator to their own experiences of drawing and painting pictures.

Make a collection: check that your chosen author/illustrator has a large body of work and make a collection of his or her books. Order the publisher's catalogue and show the children the list of books for your particular author. This is also a good opportunity for a trip to the library to look for books and go through the process of ordering books. Display the books in the book corner and encourage children to explore them independently. Which ones do they like best?

 TIPS

Help older/able children to identify differences and similarities between the books. This is a first introduction to a writer's or illustrator's 'style'.

Contact the author: get the children to help you compose a letter directly to the author, asking for a photo and information (send the letter via the publisher). Make a poster about the author and his or her work. Include your original letter plus the author's reply. Encourage the children to make written and drawn responses to the books. Ask younger ones to talk about one of the books and scribe their words. Older ones can explore elements such as character, ending and the style of illustration.

✓ READINESS

Children of all ages can enjoy the work of a particular author/illustrator. Before being introduced to the concept of 'the author', children should have had lots of experience of stories and books.

CURRICULUM GUIDANCE

Yellow stepping stone: *show interest in illustrations and print in books*
Blue stepping stones: *have favourite books; know information can be relayed in the form of print; hold books the correct way up and turn pages*
Green stepping stone: *enjoy an increasing range of books*
ELG: *explore and experiment with sounds, words and texts*

Story structure

Story structure is all about how a story is put together and what makes it a story, rather than just a written description. Character, plot, endings and settings are just some of the narrative elements that you can explore with young children.

Character

Although the main character of a story tends to be obvious to the adult or older child, younger children need to have their attention drawn to who the story is 'about'. Try some of the following activities to highlight the main character:

Character posters

Choose a story with an appealing central character – for example, the caterpillar from Eric Carle's *The Very Hungry Caterpillar* (Puffin). Use painting and collage to decorate a large drawing of the caterpillar. Look at the pictures in the book and encourage the children to choose appropriate colours and materials. Ask the children to think of words and sentences that link with the character. For the *very hungry caterpillar*, this might include *green*; *bumpy*; *hairy*; *the caterpillar likes apples*. Focus on the children's emotional reaction to the character – '*I like the very hungry caterpillar because … I think the caterpillar is funny because…*'. Stick the words and sentences around the picture of the character. Once you have made a few character posters, encourage the children to come up with their own ideas.

Character collections

Choose a character that appears in a number of books, such as David McKee's *Elmer the Patchwork Elephant* (Red Fox). Look out for Elmer in each story and make a display based on the character. Include a character poster and a collection of Elmer stories. If, like Elmer, a storybook character has been merchandised, you can also add items such as pencil cases and soft toys.

Character role play

When you carry out an organized role-play session based on a particular book (see **Role play** below), highlight the central role of the main character. Choose dressing up clothes and props to help the main character stand out and give different children the opportunity to play the character. After the role play, put out the dressing up clothes and props along with the book in the book corner.

✓ READINESS

Children of all ages can contribute to a **Character poster** and enjoy **Character collections**. In order to fully grasp the concept of character as a part of story structure, children need to have had a wide experience of books.

CURRICULUM GUIDANCE

Yellow stepping stone: *begin to be aware of the way stories are structured*

Blue stepping stone: *have favourite books*

Green stepping stone: *enjoy an increasing range of books*

ELG: *explore and experiment with sounds, words and texts*

ELG: *show an understanding of the main elements of stories, such as main character...*

NLS/TEXT: *be aware of story structures; use experience of stories ... as a basis for independent writing.*

Story settings

Once the children know a story well, focus their attention on its setting. Look at the pictures in the book and talk about the different features of the setting – fields, trees, roads, houses, sky, furniture. What visual clues might tell the children whether a story is set in the town, the home or even under water? Try the following activities to help children explore different story settings:

■ Make a labelled display of books grouped according to their settings – the countryside; the town; the home.

■ Link the concept of story settings with the children's own experiences by looking at settings for the events in their own lives – playing on the climbing frame *in the garden*; shopping with mummy *in the supermarket*; cooking on the toy cooker *in the home corner*. Photograph the children in the different settings, ask them to help you write captions for the photos and make them into a 'settings' book.

■ Create play settings for different stories. For example, turn the sand box into a farmyard setting for Pat Hutchins' *Rosie's Walk* (Puffin): set a water-filled bowl into the sand to make the pond, add a pile of straw for the haystack and so on. Encourage the children to come up with their own ideas. How could they represent the bee hives or the fence? Provide plastic models of a hen and a fox and leave the children to explore the story in their own way.

■ Chart the settings for the different events of a story. For example, a map for *Rosie's Walk* might track her route around the farmyard, showing the yard, the pond and so on.

TIPS

Choose some books with settings that represent the children's life experiences and some books that introduce new environments.

READINESS

Children of all ages can play with story settings, explore the settings for events in their everyday lives and look for the features of a setting in a picture. In order to grasp the concept of the setting as a part of story structure, children need to have had a wide experience of books.

CURRICULUM GUIDANCE

Yellow stepping stone: *begin to be aware of the way stories are structured*

Blue stepping stone: *have favourite books*

Green stepping stone: *enjoy an increasing range of books*

ELG: *explore and experiment with sounds, words and texts*

ELG: *retell narratives in the correct sequence ...*

ELG: *show an understanding of the main elements of stories ...*

NLS/TEXT: *be aware of story structures; use experience of stories ... as a basis for independent writing, e.g. retelling, substitution, extension ...*

Plot

'The plot' is what happens in a story – the sequence of events, cause and effect scenarios, actions and reactions and how the story progresses towards its eventual conclusion.

Role play

An organized role-play session is one of the best ways of helping children to explore the plot of a story. Choose a book with a clear, simple structure, such as John Burningham's *Mr Gumpy's Outing* (Jonathan Cape), and read it several times so that the children are familiar with the plot. Although the following role-play procedure is based on *Mr*

Gumpy's Outing, it provides a template for the kind of planning that is needed for any organized role-play session:

- Make a list of the different characters and the order in which they appear: Mr Gumpy (main character), the children, the rabbit and so on.

- Note down some possible actions and words for each character.

- Prepare the props: represent the boat with mats; gather together a cap and a punting pole for Mr Gumpy and clothes for the children.

- As part of an art activity, make collage ears for the animals and attach them to circular bands of card so they can be worn like a crown.

- Find each animal in the book and look at them with the children. Explain any unfamiliar actions such as *bleat* or *squabble*.

- Link the characters' behaviour with the children's own experiences. Do they ever 'squabble' like the children in the story? Do any children have a dog and a cat? Does the dog 'tease' the cat like the animals in the story?

- Encourage the whole group to practise the different actions and noises – Mr Gumpy using his punting pole, the chickens flapping and squawking, falling into the water with a splash.

- Assign the different roles: choose an older child for the central role of Mr Gumpy; let younger children play the same animal alongside a more experienced actor.

- With the children, decide on the wording for the role play. Are they going to use the same words as those in the book or come up with different statements?

- Start the role play by positioning Mr Gumpy beside the boat. Invite the animals to approach Mr Gumpy, one by one, to ask for a ride and get into the boat.

- In the story, all the animals kick, flap and trample at the same time. A large group can be easier to manage if each animal performs its action individually, before falling into the water.

- Make the most of the ending to settle any children who have become over-excited. Finish off quietly with everyone sitting down for tea.

- As the role play progresses, remember that the main focus is 'the plot'. Emphasize the sequence of events with each animal coming up to Mr Gumpy, one after the other, to ask for a ride. Highlight the cause and effect scenario, where the boat tips over *because* the animals misbehave.

★ TIPS

Ask an assistant to help model the role play, particularly if you have children who are reserved, or not very experienced with role play.

Assign roles carefully; for example, it is best not to choose the 'kicking goat' role for a child who has difficulty controlling movements or who tends to get over-excited.

This is quite a long role play. If necessary, build it up over a series of sessions. If you don't feel the group has the concentration to do the whole story, limit the number of animals.

Although this is a structured, adult-led role play, allow children the freedom to develop it in their own way.

Exploring endings

'The ending' is one of the narrative elements that turns a collection of events into a proper story. Help children to focus on endings by highlighting the conclusion of a role play, or a *Recounting stories* activity. You can also try making up some different endings for a familiar story. The following scenario is based on Eric Carle's *The Very Hungry Caterpillar*, but you can use any story with a distinctive ending that lends itself to being adapted or changed:

- Ask the children to tell you what happens at the end of *The Very Hungry Caterpillar*. Talk about the ending – were the children surprised to see what the caterpillar had turned into? Compare the caterpillar at the beginning of the story and the end of the story.

- Ask the children to think up some different endings. Prompt them if necessary – perhaps the caterpillar turns into a different creature altogether after nibbling his way out of the cocoon? Perhaps he flutters away to look for some butterfly friends?

- Use *Dictation* techniques (pages 66–7) to record each ending, encouraging emergent writers to write their own endings.

- Ask each child to illustrate his or her ending and make the alternative endings into a book. Head each ending with the child's name: *Rasa's Ending*; *Jacob's Ending*.

- Get the children to help you with wording the introduction to the book: *We have made up some new endings for 'The Very Hungry Caterpillar'*.

- Display your 'endings' book in the book corner, along with a copy of *The Very Hungry Caterpillar*.

Recounting stories

Apart from exploring story plots and endings through role play, children should also be encouraged to retell a favourite story in their own words. Once they know a book well, ask them if they can remember what happens in the story. Ask leading questions: '*What happens at the beginning of the story? What happens next? Can you remember what Mr Gumpy said to the children when they got into the boat?*' Encourage the children to check the book if they need some prompting. You can also introduce the following:

- **Puppets and soft toys:** provide puppets and toys to represent the different characters in the story. For example, use a puppet for Mr Gumpy and soft toys for the rabbit, the dog and the other animals.

- ■ **Props:** give the children items to help them recount the story. For example, the very hungry caterpillar's menu for the week – apples, pears, plums and so on.

- ■ **Storyboards:** make your own storyboard by drawing and cutting out characters from card, attaching magnetic tape to the back and using them on a magnetic board. Alternatively, make characters from felt, stick Velcro hooks to the back and use them on a felt-covered board.

⭐ TIPS

Encourage children to use storybook language, such as *Once upon a time ...; far, far away ...; and they all lived happily ever after ...*

Choose stories to reflect the cultural backgrounds of the children in your group, as well as introducing children to new and different cultures.

Use the children's words to compose a caption for each story event and ask them to draw or paint pictures. The captioned pictures can then be displayed as a wall frieze.

Older children can draw their own storyboard characters and make puppets using wooden spoons.

Check that your storyboard characters are well constructed so that the children can use them independently.

✓ READINESS

Even the youngest children can join in with **Role play**, as long as they are given the necessary support. In order to participate fully in **Exploring endings** and **Recounting stories**, children need to be able to remember the events of a story and express themselves. Children of all ages can play with and explore the story props.

CURRICULUM GUIDANCE

Yellow stepping stone: *begin to be aware of the way stories are structured*

Blue stepping stone: *have favourite books*

Green stepping stone: *enjoy an increasing range of books*

ELG: *explore and experiment with sounds, words and texts*

ELG: *retell narratives in the correct sequence, drawing on language patterns of stories*

ELG: *show an understanding of the main elements of stories, such as ... sequence of events, and openings ...*

NLS/TEXT: *be aware of story structures e.g. actions/reactions, consequences and the ways that stories are built up and concluded; use experience of stories ... as a basis for independent writing, e.g. retelling, substitution, extension ...*

Useful Resources

The following can be used to explore the many different elements of books:

Novelty books

Dorling Kindersley publish a wide range of novelty books, including books with textures, scented pages and microchip sounds (see **Useful Addresses**, pages 126–7, for contact details).

Different formats

The following are published in hardback and/or paperback, big book and/or board book formats:

- *Brown Bear, Brown Bear What Do You See?* Eric Carle and Bill Martin Jr. (Puffin)

- *Peepo!* Janet and Allan Ahlberg (Puffin)

- *Bear Hunt* Anthony Browne (Puffin)

Main character

- The Alfie stories by Shirley Hughes (Red Fox)

- The Little Princess stories by Tony Ross (Red Fox)

- *Six Dinner Sid* Inga Moore (Hodder)

Plot

- *We're Going on a Bear Hunt* Helen Oxenbury and Michael Rosen (Walker)

- *Handa's Surprise* Eileen Browne (Walker)

- *Where the Wild Things Are* Maurice Sendak (Red Fox)

Endings

- *The Tiger Who Came to Tea* Judith Kerr (Collins)

- *I Don't Want To Go To Bed* Julie Sykes and Tim Warnes (Little Tiger)

- *Owl Babies* Martin Waddell (Walker)

►

Settings

- The Lucy and Tom stories by Shirley Hughes (Puffin)

- The Katie Morag Stories by Mairi Hedderwick (Random House)

- From Dawn to Dusk series (Frances Lincoln), including:

  - ***Geeta's Day*** Prodeepta Das (Indian village)
  - ***Yikang's Day*** Sungwan So (Chinese city)

Available from: OXFAM

Planning and Recording

In this chapter ...

Assessing and recording each child's individual progress is essential to planning appropriate learning opportunities. This chapter focuses on the following areas:

- Planning

- The Early Learning Goals for literacy

- Assessment

- Record keeping.

The various suggestions can be used as they stand, or adapted to fit in with your preferred approach to planning and assessment.

Planning for literacy in the early years setting

Planning supportive and valuable learning experiences in the early years setting is a complex process. The following are just some of the main planning elements you need to consider.

The learning environment

For ideas on planning a print-rich environment and offering literacy experiences through play, see the **Organizing the setting** section in Chapter 1.

Long-term planning

Your long-term plans will depend on a number of factors, including: age range; ability levels and additional needs within your group; whether you have children with English as a second language; and the number of hours children spend in your setting. Half-termly, termly and annual plans will provide you with broad aims for each child and for the group as a whole.

Individual weekly plan

Each child should have an individual plan for the week, with space for recording learning outcomes and follow-up strategies. **Photocopiable Sheet 1: Individual Literacy Plan** can be used as a template for planning a week's worth of literacy activities for each child. Apart from the obvious headings, the record should be filled in as follows:

- ■ **EAL (English as an additional language):** make a note of the child's home language and include support strategies as part of the child's learning plan.

- ■ **Additional needs/Additional support strategies:** make a note of any additional needs and build the child's requirements into your planning.

- ■ **Observation:** record how the child responded to the activity.

- ■ **Outcome:** record what the child learned, what needs to be reinforced and appropriate follow-up activities.

If you find that you are overwhelmed with paperwork, the **Individual Literacy Plan** can be adapted for a group of children who are all at a similar level.

Planning literacy activities

Each activity should be carefully planned in advance, to ensure that it runs smoothly. Every practitioner will have their own methods of planning, but the following headings can be used as a general guide:

- ✓ **Name of activity**
- ✓ **Resources**
- ✓ **Children in group**
- ✓ **Approximate starting time/duration of activity**
- ✓ **Objectives:** for example, *learning to associate the letters b, i and t with their sounds*
- ✓ **Stepping Stones/Early Learning Goals/NLS statements:** show how the activity links with the relevant goals/NLS statements, where necessary
- ✓ **Organization of activity:** introducing the activity, what to do, key words and phrases, concluding the activity
- ✓ **Assessment questions and evidence:** what to look out for to tell you whether a child has achieved the objective. For example, can the child give you the correct letters when you say the sounds *b, t* and *i*?

Photocopiable Sheet 1: Individual Literacy Plan

INDIVIDUAL LITERACY PLAN

Key worker .... Week beginning ....

Child's name .... Age .... years .... months

EAL .... Additional needs ....

Activity	Observation	Outcome
	/	/
	/	/
	/	/
	/	/
	/	/
	/	/
	/	/
	/	/
	/	/
	/	/
	/	/
	/	/
	/	/

Additional support strategies

....

....

....

....

....

Developing Literacy Skills in the Early Years © Hilary White, 2005.

✓ **Foundation Stage Profile:** can the activity help you fill out the QCA (2003), *Foundation Stage Profile?*

✓ **Differentiation/Additional needs:** plan how you intend to cater for different age groups/ability levels and additional needs within the group

✓ **Observations:** record how the activity went and how you could improve on it next time.

Meeting the Early Learning Goals

As part of your planning, it is important to check that you are addressing all the Stepping Stones and working towards the Early Learning Goals from the QCA (2000), *Curriculum Guidance for the Foundation Stage.* The following charts link the activities in this book with the appropriate ELGs and Stepping Stones for 'Linking sounds and letters', 'Handwriting', 'Writing' and 'Reading'. Relevant statements from *The National Literacy Strategy Framework* (DfEE, 1998) are also included in the charts.

To help with assessment, each activity in the charts has a bracketed code to show whether it can be used as evidence towards filling in the QCA *Foundation Stage Profile.* The letters of the code represent the different sections of the Profile:

■ **PL = Linking sounds and letters** section

■ **PR = Reading** section

■ **PW = Writing** section.

Each code is also numbered to match the statements in the Profile record booklet. For example, **PR1** represents the first statement in the **Reading** section.

The charts (pages 111–18) can be photocopied for planning and recording purposes.

Assessment questions

Detailed and thorough assessment is necessary to map the child's progress, and to provide the basis for planning. The following questions offer some broad guidelines for assessing the development of literacy skills. The questions relate to the different sections in each chapter of this book and, where relevant, they are referenced to a particular activity.

Each question is coded so that it can be linked with the QCA (2003) *Foundation Stage Profile* (see above for an explanation of the code).

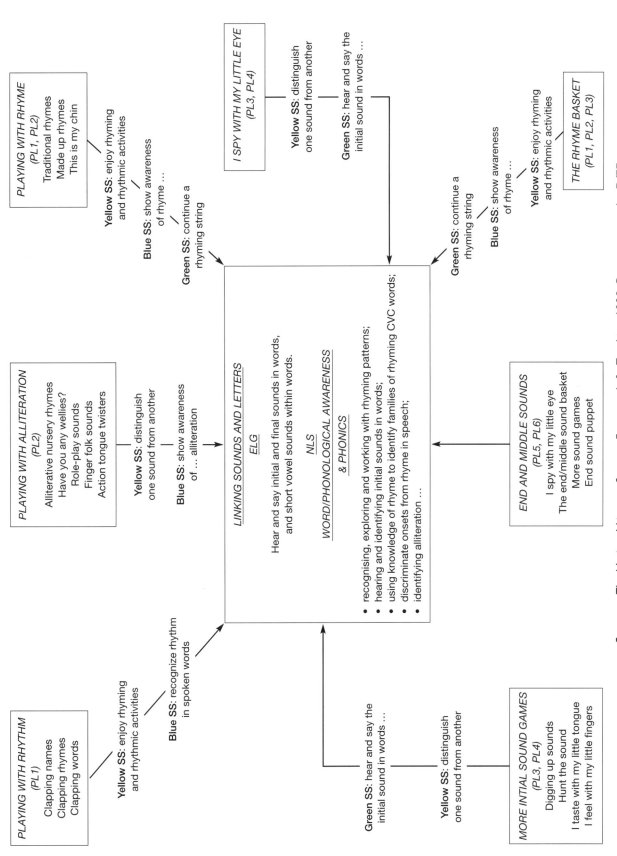

PLAYING WITH RHYME
(PL1, PL2)
Traditional rhymes
Made up rhymes
This is my chin

Yellow SS: enjoy rhyming and rhythmic activities

Blue SS: show awareness of rhyme …

Green SS: continue a rhyming string

I SPY WITH MY LITTLE EYE
(PL3, PL4)

Yellow SS: distinguish one sound from another

Green SS: hear and say the initial sound in words …

THE RHYME BASKET
(PL1, PL2, PL3)

Green SS: continue a rhyming string

Blue SS: show awareness of rhyme …

Yellow SS: enjoy rhyming and rhythmic activities

PLAYING WITH ALLITERATION
(PL2)
Alliterative nursery rhymes
Have you any wellies?
Role-play sounds
Finger folk sounds
Action tongue twisters

Yellow SS: distinguish one sound from another

Blue SS: show awareness of … alliteration

LINKING SOUNDS AND LETTERS
<u>ELG</u>

Hear and say initial and final sounds in words, and short vowel sounds within words.

<u>NLS</u>
<u>WORD/PHONOLOGICAL AWARENESS</u>
<u>& PHONICS</u>

- recognising, exploring and working with rhyming patterns;
- hearing and identifying initial sounds in words;
- using knowledge of rhyme to identify families of rhyming CVC words;
- discriminate onsets from rhyme in speech;
- identifying alliteration …

END AND MIDDLE SOUNDS
(PL5, PL6)
I spy with my little eye
The end/middle sound basket
More sound games
End sound puppet

PLAYING WITH RHYTHM
(PL1)
Clapping names
Clapping rhymes
Clapping words

Yellow SS: enjoy rhyming and rhythmic activities

Blue SS: recognize rhythm in spoken words

Green SS: hear and say the initial sound in words …

Yellow SS: distinguish one sound from another

MORE INTIAL SOUND GAMES
(PL3, PL4)
Digging up sounds
Hunt the sound
I taste with my little tongue
I feel with my little fingers

Sources: *The National Literacy Strategy Framework for Teaching*, 1998 Crown copyright, DfEE Publications and *Curriculum Guidance for the Foundation Stage*, 2000 copyright QCA publications

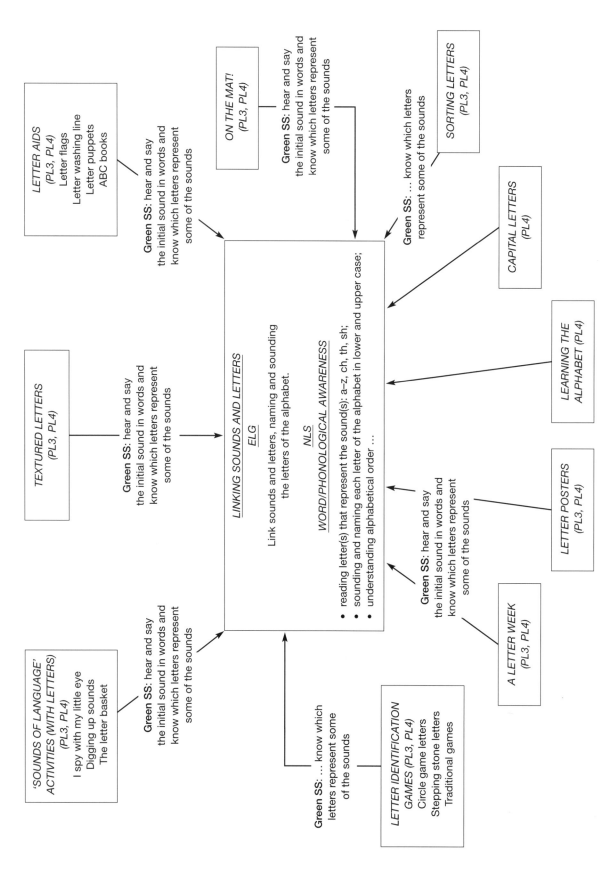

LETTER AIDS
(PL3, PL4)
Letter flags
Letter washing line
Letter puppets
ABC books

Green SS: hear and say the initial sound in words and know which letters represent some of the sounds

ON THE MAT!
(PL3, PL4)

Green SS: hear and say the initial sound in words and know which letters represent some of the sounds

SORTING LETTERS
(PL3, PL4)

Green SS: ... know which letters represent some of the sounds

CAPITAL LETTERS
(PL4)

TEXTURED LETTERS
(PL3, PL4)

Green SS: hear and say the initial sound in words and know which letters represent some of the sounds

LINKING SOUNDS AND LETTERS
ELG

Link sounds and letters, naming and sounding the letters of the alphabet.

NLS
WORD/PHONOLOGICAL AWARENESS

- reading letter(s) that represent the sound(s): a–z, ch, th, sh;
- sounding and naming each letter of the alphabet in lower and upper case;
- understanding alphabetical order ...

LEARNING THE ALPHABET *(PL4)*

LETTER POSTERS
(PL3, PL4)

Green SS: hear and say the initial sound in words and know which letters represent some of the sounds

A LETTER WEEK
(PL3, PL4)

'SOUNDS OF LANGUAGE' ACTIVITIES (WITH LETTERS)
(PL3, PL4)
I spy with my little eye
Digging up sounds
The letter basket

Green SS: hear and say the initial sound in words and know which letters represent some of the sounds

Green SS: ... know which letters represent some of the sounds

LETTER IDENTIFICATION
GAMES *(PL3, PL4)*
Circle game letters
Stepping stone letters
Traditional games

Sources: *The National Literacy Strategy Framework for Teaching*, 1998 Crown copyright, DfEE Publications and *Curriculum Guidance for the Foundation Stage*, 2000 copyright QCA publications

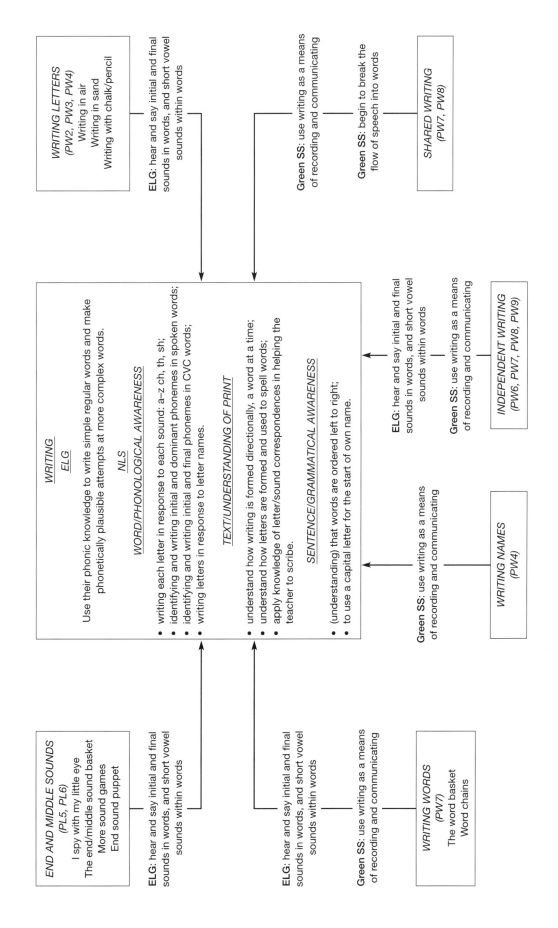

WRITING LETTERS
(PW2, PW3, PW4)
Writing in air
Writing in sand
Writing with chalk/pencil

ELG: hear and say initial and final sounds in words, and short vowel sounds within words

Green SS: use writing as a means of recording and communicating

Green SS: begin to break the flow of speech into words

SHARED WRITING
(PW7, PW8)

WRITING
ELG

Use their phonic knowledge to write simple regular words and make phonetically plausible attempts at more complex words.

NLS

WORD/PHONOLOGICAL AWARENESS

- writing each letter in response to each sound: a–z ch, th, sh;
- identifying and writing initial and dominant phonemes in spoken words;
- identifying and writing initial and final phonemes in CVC words;
- writing letters in response to letter names.

TEXT/UNDERSTANDING OF PRINT

- understand how writing is formed directionally, a word at a time;
- understand how letters are formed and used to spell words;
- apply knowledge of letter/sound correspondences in helping the teacher to scribe.

SENTENCE/GRAMMATICAL AWARENESS

- (understanding) that words are ordered left to right;
- to use a capital letter for the start of own name.

ELG: hear and say initial and final sounds in words, and short vowel sounds within words

Green SS: use writing as a means of recording and communicating

INDEPENDENT WRITING
(PW6, PW7, PW8, PW9)

Green SS: use writing as a means of recording and communicating

WRITING NAMES
(PW4)

END AND MIDDLE SOUNDS
(PL5, PL6)
I spy with my little eye
The end/middle sound basket
More sound games
End sound puppet

ELG: hear and say initial and final sounds in words, and short vowel sounds within words

ELG: hear and say initial and final sounds in words, and short vowel sounds within words

Green SS: use writing as a means of recording and communicating

WRITING WORDS
(PW7)
The word basket
Word chains

Sources: *The National Literacy Strategy Framework for Teaching*, 1998 Crown copyright, DfEE Publications and *Curriculum Guidance for the Foundation Stage*, 2000 copyright QCA publications

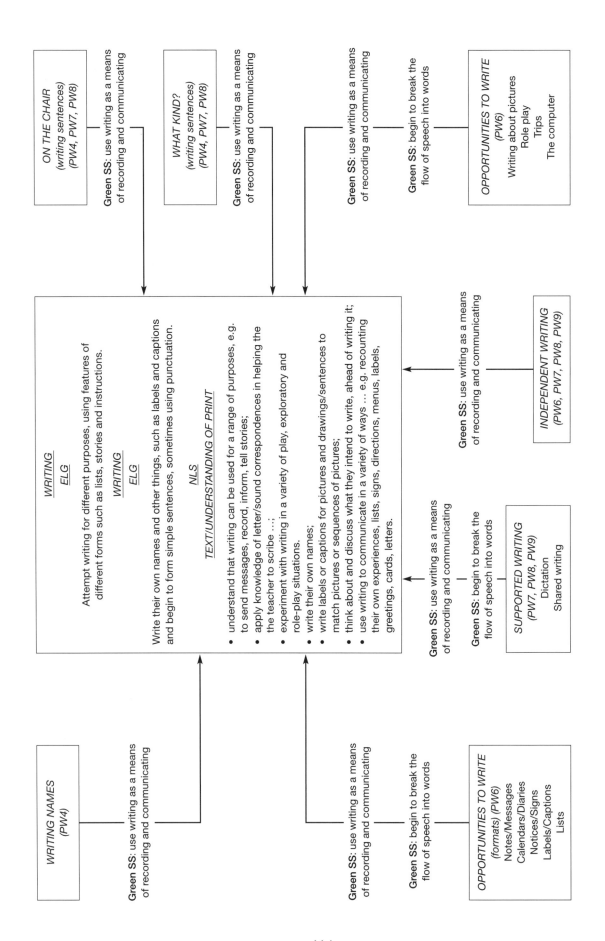

ON THE CHAIR
(writing sentences)
(PW4, PW7, PW8)

Green SS: use writing as a means of recording and communicating

WHAT KIND?
(writing sentences)
(PW4, PW7, PW8)

Green SS: use writing as a means of recording and communicating

Green SS: use writing as a means of recording and communicating

Green SS: begin to break the flow of speech into words

OPPORTUNITIES TO WRITE
(PW6)
Writing about pictures
Role play
Trips
The computer

WRITING
ELG

Attempt writing for different purposes, using features of different forms such as lists, stories and instructions.

WRITING
ELG

Write their own names and other things, such as labels and captions and begin to form simple sentences, sometimes using punctuation.

NLS

TEXT/UNDERSTANDING OF PRINT

• understand that writing can be used for a range of purposes, e.g. to send messages, record, inform, tell stories;
• apply knowledge of letter/sound correspondences in helping the teacher to scribe …;
• experiment with writing in a variety of play, exploratory and role-play situations.
• write their own names;
• write labels or captions for pictures and drawings/sentences to match pictures or sequences of pictures;
• think about and discuss what they intend to write, ahead of writing it; use writing to communicate in a variety of ways … e.g. recounting their own experiences, lists, signs, directions, menus, labels, greetings, cards, letters.

Green SS: use writing as a means of recording and communicating

INDEPENDENT WRITING
(PW6, PW7, PW8, PW9)

Green SS: use writing as a means of recording and communicating

Green SS: begin to break the flow of speech into words

SUPPORTED WRITING
(PW7, PW8, PW9)
Dictation
Shared writing

WRITING NAMES
(PW4)

Green SS: use writing as a means of recording and communicating

Green SS: use writing as a means of recording and communicating

Green SS: begin to break the flow of speech into words

OPPORTUNITIES TO WRITE
(formats) (PW6)
Notes/Messages
Calendars/Diaries
Notices/Signs
Labels/Captions
Lists

Sources: *The National Literacy Strategy Framework for Teaching,* 1998 Crown copyright, DfEE Publications and *Curriculum Guidance for the Foundation Stage,* 2000 copyright QCA publications

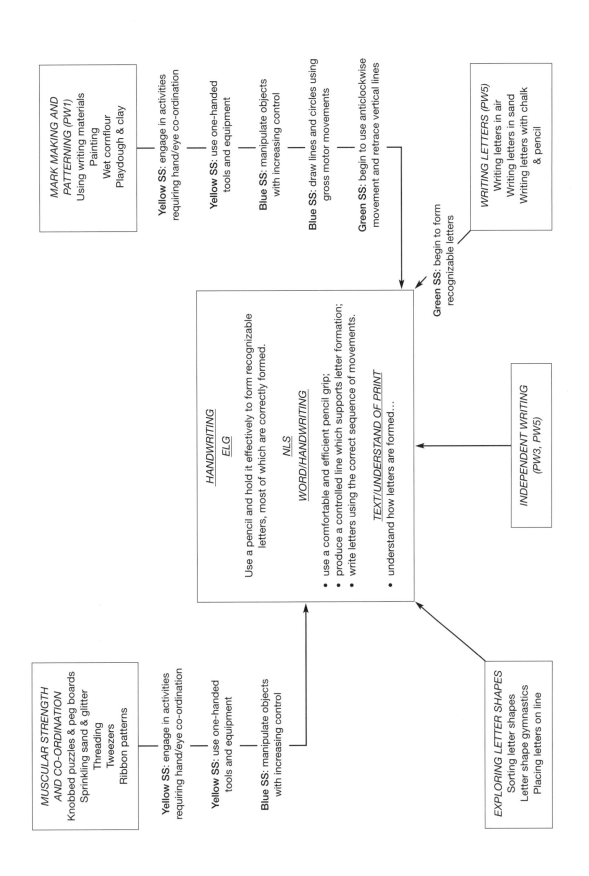

MARK MAKING AND PATTERNING (PW1)
Using writing materials
Painting
Wet cornflour
Playdough & clay

Yellow SS: engage in activities requiring hand/eye co-ordination

Yellow SS: use one-handed tools and equipment

Blue SS: manipulate objects with increasing control

Blue SS: draw lines and circles using gross motor movements

Green SS: begin to use anticlockwise movement and retrace vertical lines

WRITING LETTERS (PW5)
Writing letters in air
Writing letters in sand
Writing letters with chalk & pencil

Green SS: begin to form recognizable letters

HANDWRITING
ELG

Use a pencil and hold it effectively to form recognizable letters, most of which are correctly formed.

NLS
WORD/HANDWRITING

- use a comfortable and efficient pencil grip;
- produce a controlled line which supports letter formation;
- write letters using the correct sequence of movements.

TEXT/UNDERSTAND OF PRINT

- understand how letters are formed...

INDEPENDENT WRITING
(PW3, PW5)

MUSCULAR STRENGTH AND CO-ORDINATION
Knobbed puzzles & peg boards
Sprinkling sand & glitter
Threading
Tweezers
Ribbon patterns

Yellow SS: engage in activities requiring hand/eye co-ordination

Yellow SS: use one-handed tools and equipment

Blue SS: manipulate objects with increasing control

EXPLORING LETTER SHAPES
Sorting letter shapes
Letter shape gymnastics
Placing letters on line

Sources: _The National Literacy Strategy Framework for Teaching_, 1998 Crown copyright, DfEE Publications and _Curriculum Guidance for the Foundation Stage_, 2000 copyright QCA publications

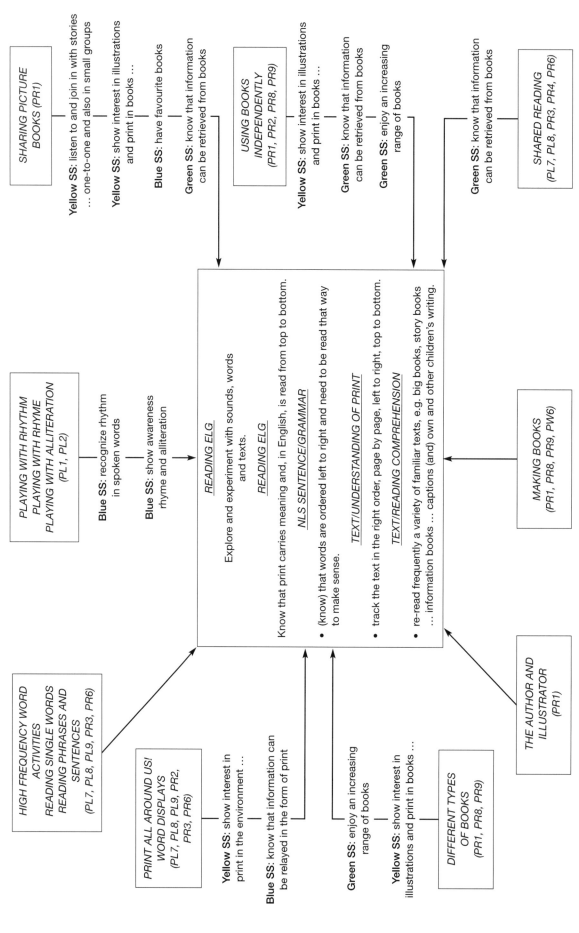

SHARING PICTURE BOOKS (PR1)

Yellow SS: listen to and join in with stories … one-to-one and also in small groups

Yellow SS: show interest in illustrations and print in books …

Blue SS: have favourite books

Green SS: know that information can be retrieved from books

USING BOOKS INDEPENDENTLY (PR1, PR2, PR8, PR9)

Yellow SS: show interest in illustrations and print in books …

Green SS: know that information can be retrieved from books

Green SS: enjoy an increasing range of books

Green SS: know that information can be retrieved from books

SHARED READING (PL7, PL8, PR3, PR4, PR6)

PLAYING WITH RHYTHM PLAYING WITH RHYME PLAYING WITH ALLITERATION (PL1, PL2)

Blue SS: recognize rhythm in spoken words

Blue SS: show awareness rhyme and alliteration

READING ELG

Explore and experiment with sounds, words and texts.

READING ELG

NLS SENTENCE/GRAMMAR

Know that print carries meaning and, in English, is read from top to bottom.

TEXT/UNDERSTANDING OF PRINT

- (know) that words are ordered left to right and need to be read that way to make sense.

- track the text in the right order, page by page, left to right, top to bottom.

TEXT/READING COMPREHENSION

- re-read frequently a variety of familiar texts, e.g. big books, story books … information books … captions (and) own and other children's writing.

MAKING BOOKS (PR1, PR8, PR9, PW6)

HIGH FREQUENCY WORD ACTIVITIES READING SINGLE WORDS READING PHRASES AND SENTENCES (PL7, PL8, PL9, PR3, PR6)

PRINT ALL AROUND US! WORD DISPLAYS (PL7, PL8, PL9, PR2, PR3, PR6)

Yellow SS: show interest in print in the environment …

Blue SS: know that information can be relayed in the form of print

Green SS: enjoy an increasing range of books

Yellow SS: show interest in illustrations and print in books …

THE AUTHOR AND ILLUSTRATOR (PR1)

DIFFERENT TYPES OF BOOKS (PR1, PR8, PR9)

Sources: *The National Literacy Strategy Framework for Teaching*, 1998 Crown copyright, DfEE Publications and *Curriculum Guidance for the Foundation Stage*, 2000 copyright QCA publications

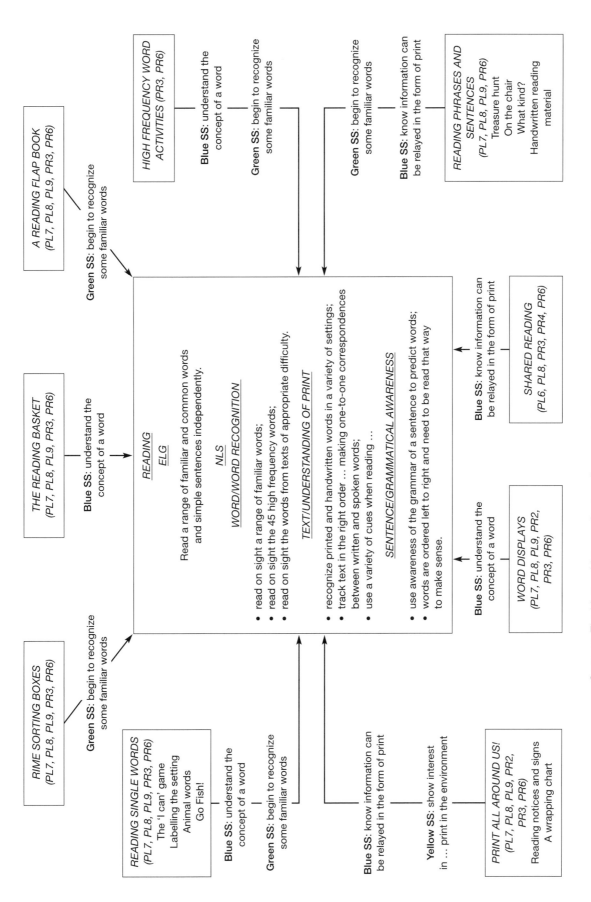

A READING FLAP BOOK
(PL7, PL8, PL9, PR3, PR6)

Green SS: begin to recognize some familiar words

HIGH FREQUENCY WORD ACTIVITIES (PR3, PR6)

Blue SS: understand the concept of a word

Green SS: begin to recognize some familiar words

Green SS: begin to recognize some familiar words

Blue SS: know information can be relayed in the form of print

READING PHRASES AND SENTENCES
(PL7, PL8, PL9, PR6)
Treasure hunt
On the chair
What kind?
Handwritten reading material

THE READING BASKET
(PL7, PL8, PL9, PR3, PR6)

Blue SS: understand the concept of a word

<u>READING</u>
<u>ELG</u>

Read a range of familiar and common words and simple sentences independently.

<u>NLS</u>
<u>WORD/WORD RECOGNITION</u>

- read on sight a range of familiar words;
- read on sight the 45 high frequency words;
- read on sight the words from texts of appropriate difficulty.

<u>TEXT/UNDERSTANDING OF PRINT</u>

- recognize printed and handwritten words in a variety of settings;
- track text in the right order … making one-to-one correspondences between written and spoken words;
- use a variety of cues when reading …

<u>SENTENCE/GRAMMATICAL AWARENESS</u>

- use awareness of the grammar of a sentence to predict words;
- words are ordered left to right and need to be read that way to make sense.

Blue SS: know information can be relayed in the form of print

SHARED READING
(PL6, PL8, PR3, PR4, PR6)

Blue SS: understand the concept of a word

WORD DISPLAYS
(PL7, PL8, PL9, PR2, PR3, PR6)

RIME SORTING BOXES
(PL7, PL8, PL9, PR3, PR6)

Green SS: begin to recognize some familiar words

READING SINGLE WORDS
(PL7, PL8, PL9, PR3, PR6)
The 'I can' game
Labelling the setting
Animal words
Go Fish!

Blue SS: understand the concept of a word

Green SS: begin to recognize some familiar words

Blue SS: know information can be relayed in the form of print

Yellow SS: show interest in … print in the environment

PRINT ALL AROUND US!
(PL7, PL8, PL9, PR2, PR3, PR6)
Reading notices and signs
A wrapping chart

Sources: *The National Literacy Strategy Framework for Teaching,* 1998 Crown copyright, DfEE Publications and *Curriculum Guidance for the Foundation Stage,* 2000 copyright QCA publications

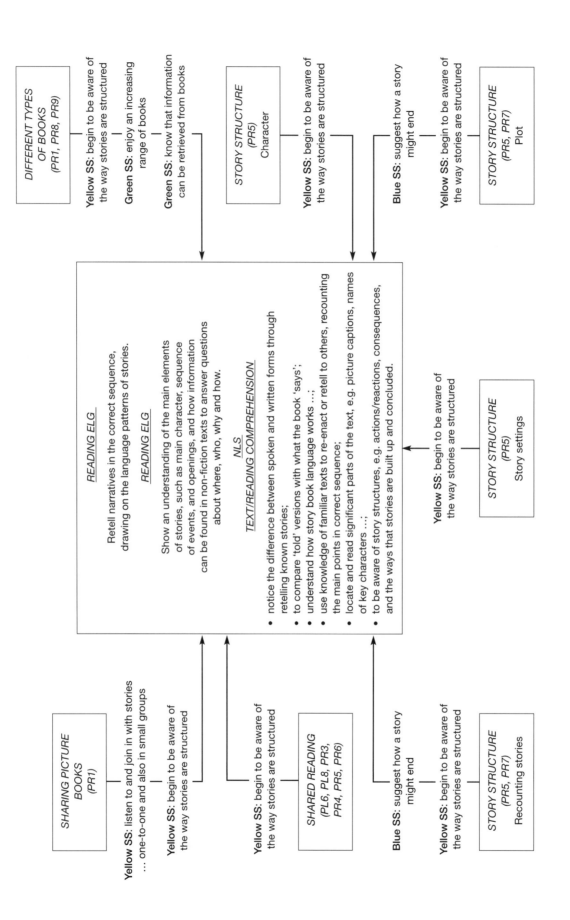

DIFFERENT TYPES OF BOOKS
(PR1, PR8, PR9)

Yellow SS: begin to be aware of the way stories are structured

Green SS: enjoy an increasing range of books

Green SS: know that information can be retrieved from books

STORY STRUCTURE
(PR5)
Character

Yellow SS: begin to be aware of the way stories are structured

Blue SS: suggest how a story might end

Yellow SS: begin to be aware of the way stories are structured

STORY STRUCTURE
(PR5, PR7)
Plot

READING ELG

Retell narratives in the correct sequence, drawing on the language patterns of stories.

READING ELG

Show an understanding of the main elements of stories, such as main character, sequence of events, and openings, and how information can be found in non-fiction texts to answer questions about where, who, why and how.

NLS
TEXT/READING COMPREHENSION

- notice the difference between spoken and written forms through retelling known stories;
- to compare 'told' versions with what the book 'says';
- understand how story book language works ...;
- use knowledge of familiar texts to re-enact or retell to others, recounting the main points in correct sequence;
- locate and read significant parts of the text, e.g. picture captions, names of key characters ...;
- to be aware of story structures, e.g. actions/reactions, consequences, and the ways that stories are built up and concluded.

Yellow SS: begin to be aware of the way stories are structured

STORY STRUCTURE
(PR5)
Story settings

SHARING PICTURE BOOKS
(PR1)

Yellow SS: listen to and join in with stories ... one-to-one and also in small groups

Yellow SS: begin to be aware of the way stories are structured

Yellow SS: begin to be aware of the way stories are structured

SHARED READING
(PL6, PL8, PR3, PR4, PR5, PR6)

Blue SS: suggest how a story might end

Yellow SS: begin to be aware of the way stories are structured

STORY STRUCTURE
(PR5, PR7)
Recounting stories

Sources: *The National Literacy Strategy Framework for Teaching*, 1998 Crown copyright, DfEE Publications and *Curriculum Guidance for the Foundation Stage*, 2000 copyright QCA publications

Chapter 2: The Sounds of Language

Rhythm and rhyme

Are the children able to join in with clapping a rhythm? Can they reproduce the rhythm and start creating their own rhythms? (**PL1**)

Can children fill in the missing rhyming word in a familiar nursery rhyme? Can they think of their own rhyming words? Can they hear the rhyme in a string of rhyming words and group words according to rhyme? (see **The rhyme basket**, pages 24–6)? (**PL2**)

Initial sounds/Middle and end sounds

Can the children repeat the initial sound of a word? Can they detect it independently? Can they hear the end sound of a word? (**PL5**) Can they hear the middle sound of a CVC word? Can they analyse all the sounds in a CVC word? (**PL6**) Can they analyse the sounds in a longer word? The different stages of *I spy* (pages 29–34) can help you judge which stage each child has reached.

Chapter 3: Matching Sound and Symbol

Introducing letters

Can children correctly link sounds with the 26 letters of the alphabet plus *th*, *ch* and *sh*? (**PL3**, **PL4**) Step 3 of the **Textured letters** activity (page 38) will help you to judge which letters the child knows.

Practising letters

Can children match two identical letters? Can they articulate the sound made by a letter as part of a game? Can they pick out a letter when given a sound? (**PL3**, **PL4**)

Exploring letters

Can children recognize the same letter in different print styles and sizes? Can they find letters in printed/handwritten text: with help; independently? (**PL3**, **PL4**)

The alphabet

Can children name the 26 letters of the alphabet and link corresponding lower and upper case letters? Are they starting to recognize capital letters in print and know that their name starts with a capital? Do they know the order of the alphabet? (**PL4**)

Chapter 4: Becoming a Writer

Pre-writing activities

Are children starting to produce a controlled line with a writing implement? Do they have an appropriate pencil grip? Are they deliberately making marks and patterns with paint and other substances? Are they starting to ascribe meaning to those marks? (**PW1**)

Handwriting

Can the children reproduce the letter shapes: in sand and finger paint; with a writing implement? (**PW2**, **PW3**)

Are they starting to write letters independently during play activities? (**PW2**, **PW3**)

Can they group different letter shapes, such as letters with tails? Can they place them correctly on a line: as a cut out letter; in writing? (**PW5**)

Content

Are children attempting to write their own names? Can they do so accurately, with a capital letter at the start? (**PW4**)

Can they analyse the sounds in a CVC word, choose the appropriate letters and put them in the correct order: with cut-out letters; with a writing implement? (see *The word basket*, pages 64–5) (**PW7**)

Are they showing signs of independent emergent writing during play? Can they contribute to supported writing: through *Dictation* (pages 66–7); through *Shared writing* (page 67)? (**PR2**, **PW4**, **PW5**, **PW6**, **PW7**, **PW8**, **PW9**)

Are they starting to understand the many different purposes of writing? Are they starting to understand that different formats can be used, such as lists and labels? (**PW6**, **PW8**)

Chapter 5: Becoming a Reader

The beginnings of reading

Can children sound out the letters in a CVC word and blend the sounds to read the word: with the context of an object; without the context of an object? (see *The reading basket*, pages 78–80) (**PL7**) Are they starting to read high frequency and other simple words by sight? (**PR3**, **PR6**)

Reading activities

Are children attempting to read new words? (**PL7, PL8, PL9**) Are they attempting to read sentences? Can they interpret what they have read? (**PR6**) Can they use context to help them understand meaning? At what level can they contribute to shared reading sessions? (**PL7, PL8, PL9, PR1, PR2, PR3, PR4, PR6**)

Reading in the environment

Are children starting to respond to environmental print – wrappings, signs and notices? Are they reading the print through sight recognition and/or using phonics knowledge and other reading strategies such as context? (**PL7, PL8, PL9, PR2, PR3, PR6**)

Chapter 6: The Role of the Picture Book

Exploring picture books

Do children listen attentively to a story and respond appropriately? Do they use the book corner independently? (**PR1**) Are they starting to realize that books can be used as a source of information? (**PR2, PR8, PR9**)

Making books

Can children make useful suggestions as to the content of a home-made book? (**PR5, PR7, PR8**) Can they name the different parts of a book and help to design and construct a group book? Can they draw on their knowledge of different shapes, sizes and formats in constructing their own book?

Exploring story structure

Are children starting to recognize that a story has a plot by guessing/remembering what happens next? Can they focus on a main character and recognize that character in other books? Can they identify the story setting? Can they think up new endings? (**PR5**) Are they starting to use storybook language in their own storying? (**PR7**)

Keeping records

Record keeping is essential to both planning and assessment. Use your records to assess a child's ongoing progress and decide future planning for both the individual and the group. The following elements will help to provide comprehensive literacy records:

Photocopiable Sheet 1: Individual Literacy Plan (page 109)

File your individual weekly literacy plans as an ongoing record for each child/group of children.

Photocopiable Sheet 2: Reading/Writing Snapshot (page 123)

This sheet can be photocopied and filled in periodically. Use it to record the children's developing writing skills and attitudes to books and literacy in general.

Photocopiable Sheet 3: Phonics/High Frequency Word Record (page 124)

This sheet can be photocopied and used to record the child's developing knowledge of letter/sound links and the NLS high frequency words.

✓ ***Phonics:*** place a dot beneath a letter when it has been introduced. Draw a circle around the letter once the child knows it well. Step 3 of the ***Textured letters*** activity (page 40) can be used to assess the child's knowledge of the letters.

✓ ***High frequency words:*** circle *r* when the children can read the word and *w* when they can write it.

Literacy folders

Provide each child with a sturdy card folder. Ask them to write their name on the front and decorate the folder. Put important pieces of work in the folder as a record of the child's literacy development. Name and date the work and add a written explanation of its significance. Encourage the children to choose special pieces of work to add to their folder. The folder can then be passed on to the child's next school/class teacher.

QCA Foundation Stage Profile

Draw on all your literacy records to help you complete the statutory QCA Profile for each child.

Photocopiable Sheet 2:
Reading/Writing Snapshot

Key worker .... Date ....

A READING AND WRITING SNAPSHOT FOR

....

(name)

> I can write these letters
>
>
>
>
>

> I can write these words
>
>
>
>
>

My favourite story is ....

My favourite rhyme is ....

My favourite activity is ....

> Key worker's notes and observations
>
>
>
>
>
>

Developing Literacy Skills in the Early Years, © Hilary White, 2005.

Photocopiable Sheet 3:
Phonics/High Frequency Word Record

Key worker ....

Child's name ....

Start date for record: phonics .... high frequency words ....

PHONICS RECORD

Put a dot beneath letter when it has been introduced. Circle letter when child can confidently link letter with sound

a	b	c	d	e	f	g	h	i	j
k	l	m	n	o	p	q	r	s	t
u	v	w	x	y	z	th	ch	sh	

HIGH FREQUENCY WORD RECORD

Circle *r* when child can read word and *w* when child can write word.

I *r w*   up *r w*   look *r w*   we *r w*   like *r w*   and *r w*   on *r w*

at *r w*   for *r w*   he *r w*   can *r w*   said *r w*   go *r w*   you *r w*

are *r w*   this *r w*   going *r w*   they *r w*   away *r w*   play *r w*

a *r w*   am *r w*   to *r w*   cat *r w*   come *r w*   day *r w*

the *r w*   dog *r w*   big *r w*   my *r w*   mum *r w*   no *r w*

dad *r w*   all *r w*   get *r w*   in *r w*   went *r w*   was *r w*

of *r w*   me *r w*   she *r w*   see *r w*   it *r w*   yes *r w*   is *r w*

Developing Literacy Skills in the Early Years, © Hilary White, 2005.

References and Further Reading

Beyer, J. and Gammeltoft, L. (1998) *Autism and Play*. Denmark/London: Jessica Kingsley.

Butler, D. (1980) *Babies Need Books*. London: Penguin (excellent survey of classic picture books).

Department for Education and Employment (DfEE) (1998) *The National Literacy Strategy: Framework for Teaching*. London: DfEE.

Department for Education and Skills (DfES) (2004) *Playing with Sounds: A Supplement for Progression in Phonics*. London: DfES.

Drifte, C. (2002) *Early Learning Goals for Children with Special Needs: Learning through Play*. London: David Fulton Publishers.

Griffiths, F. (2002) *Communication Counts: Speech and Language Difficulties in the Early Years*. London: David Fulton Publishers.

Harries, J. (2004) *Role Play*. Leamington Spa: Step Forward Publishing (practical role-play activities linked to the ELGs).

Makin, L. and Whitehead, M. (2004) *How to Develop Children's Early Literacy*. London: Paul Chapman Publishing.

Qualifications and Curriculum Authority (QCA) (2000) *Curriculum Guidance for the Foundation Stage*. London: QCA.

Qualifications and Curriculum Authority (QCA) (2003) *Foundation Stage Profile: Handbook*. London: QCA.

Warland, J. (2004) *Living Phonics*. Oxford: Ransom Publishing (a phonics scheme with a useful section on phoneme pronunciation).

Whitehead, M. (1997) *Language and Literacy in the Early Years*. London: Paul Chapman Publishing.

Useful Addresses

Below is a list of educational suppliers referred to in the **Useful Resources** section at the end of Chapters 2–6.

THE CONSORTIUM
Tel: 0845 330 7780
www.theconsortium.co.uk

DORLING KINDERSLEY
Tel: 020 8757 4400
www.dk.com

THE EARLY LEARNING CENTRE
Tel: 08705 352 352
www.elc.co.uk

EDUCATION SUPPLIES DIRECTORY
Tel: 0870 220 2831
www.educationsuppliesdirect.com

NES ARNOLD
Tel: 0870 6000 192
www.nesarnold.co.uk

OXFAM CATALOGUE FOR SCHOOLS
Tel: 01865 312610
www.oxfam.org.uk

PHILIP AND TACEY
Tel: 01264 332171
www.philipandtacey.co.uk

PRACTICAL PRE-SCHOOL
Tel: 01926 420046
www.practicalpreschool.com

QCA Publications
Tel: 01787 884444
www.qca.org.uk

DfES Publications
Tel: 0845 60 222 60
www.dfes.gov.uk

WESCO
Tel: 0115 986 2126
www.wesco-group.com

Glossary

alliteration: a phrase or sentence where a number of words begin with the same sound, for example *Lucy Locket lost her pocket*.

blending: the process of merging separate sounds to create a larger unit such as a cluster or a word.

cluster: a group of letters that blend together to create a sound unit, such as *air* or *str*.

consonant: a sound where the flow of air is restricted by the tongue, teeth, lips or palate. All the letters of the alphabet are consonants apart from *a, e, i, o u*, and *y* in a word such as *fly*.

consonant blend: blending two consonants together, for example *g + r = gr*.

context: the parts before and following a word or sentence. Context can help the child to read an unfamiliar word and interpret the overall meaning.

cursive script: single letters similar in appearance to the letters that are used in joined-up handwriting.

CVC words: words with a consonant-vowel-consonant structure, such as *c-a-t, d-o-g*.

digraph: the combination of two written letters to represent a single sound. For example, *th, ai, st*.

grapheme: a written letter or combination of letters representing a phoneme.

irregular words: words that cannot be sounded out using the 26 sounds of the alphabet. For example, *where, here*.

onset: the initial sound at the start of a monosyllabic word. For example, *c-* as in *cap*; *tr-* as in *trip*.

phoneme: the smallest unit of sound within a word. A phoneme may be represented by a single letter (*d-* as in *dog*), two letters (*-oo* as in *too*), three letters (*-air* as in *fair*) or four letters (*-ough* as in *through*).

phonological awareness: a sensitivity to the sounds of spoken language, including the ability to recognize and create rhyme and alliteration and detect the separate phonemes in a word.

rhyming string: a string of words that rhyme, for example *chair, bear, stare*.

rime: the vowel and end consonant or consonants of a monosyllabic word. For example, *-ig* as in *pig*; *-ath* as in *bath*.

segmenting: the process of breaking a word into its separate phonemes, prior to writing. For example, *t-r-ai-n*; *sh-or-t*.

sentence: a collection of words that make sense on their own, as opposed to a phrase. For example:

> sentence: *Tom walked to the park.*
> phrase: *to the park*

In written language, a sentence begins with a capital letter and ends with a full stop.

syllable: the beats in a word. A monosyllabic word has just one beat (*cat*), a multisyllabic word has two or more beats (*bo-ttle*; *el-e-phant*). Every syllable must contain a vowel sound.

upper case letters: capital letters.

vowels: a sound produced with very little restriction to air flow from the tongue, teeth or lips. Short vowel sounds are represented by the five vowels from the alphabet, *a* (*cat*), *e* (*peg*), *i* (*tip*), *o* (*pot*), *u* (*cup*) and *oo* as in *book*. Long vowel sounds are usually represented by a combination of vowels or vowels and consonants, for example *ea*, *ai*, *ar*, *air*.

Index

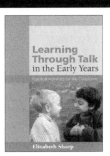

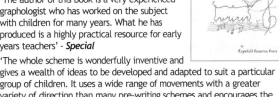

MORE LITERACY TITLES
from SAGE Publications and Paul Chapman Publishing

Language and Literacy in the Early Years
Third Edition
Marian R Whitehead *Independent Consultant, UK*

'A most useful, practical text which no early years practitioner should be without' - *Jacqueline Barbera, Director of Undergraduate ITT Liverpool Hope University College*

This **Third Edition** of **Language and Literacy in the Early Years** provides comprehensive coverage of issues in language, literacy and learning, focusing on the age range birth to eight years.

The author emphasizes the joy and creativity involved in supporting young children's development as speakers, writers and readers. While taking account of current initiatives and programmes, the author supports flexible teaching methods in what is a complex teaching and learning process.

This book is essential reading for primary and early years students and practitioners in the field of language and literacy including nursery nurses, classroom assistants and Foundation Stage teachers.

Contents
PART ONE: LANGUAGE AND LEARNING \ Linguistics \ Sociolinguistics \ Psycholinguistics \ The Early-Years Educator and Knowledge about Language \ PART TWO: LITERACY \ Narrative and Storying \ Books and the World of Literature \ Early Representation and Emerging Writing \ The Early Years Educator and Literacy

2004 • 272 pages
Cloth (0-7619-4469-9) / Paper (0-7619-4470-2)

How to Develop Children's Early Literacy
A Guide for Professional Carers and Educators

Laurie Makin *University of Newcastle, Australia* and **Marian R Whitehead** *Independent Consultant, UK*

'Laurie Makin's and Marian Whitehead's book on **How to Develop Children's Literacy** stands out from the usual guides on child development and learning. The language is accessible and engaging' - *Childforum, New Zealand*

Are you studying for a vocational qualification in early childhood? Are you a qualified teacher working with under-fives for the first time? Are you a nursery nurse or teaching assistant? Or are you thinking about doing one of these things? If so, this book is for you.

It addresses current issues relating to early literacy, and offers pragmatic ideas and information on key areas including play, bilingualism, special needs, and official curriculum frameworks.

How to Develop Children's Early Literacy is a practical guide designed to support all early literacy educators and addresses current issues relating to early literacy.

Contents
Literacy for Babies \ Literacy for Toddlers \ Literacy for Pre-School and Nursery Children \ Literacy for Children in Transition to School \ Let's Think about... \ Some Useful Resources

2003 • 122 pages
Cloth (0-7619-4332-3) / Paper (0-7619-4333-1)

Handbook of Early Childhood Literacy
Edited by **Nigel Hall** *Manchester Metropolitan University,* **Joanne Larson** *University of Rochester, New York* and **Jackie Marsh** *University of Sheffield*

'A significant resource which promises to become a landmark text' - *Eve Bearne, University of Cambridge, Faculty of Education*

This **Handbook** provides an overview of contemporary research into early childhood literacy, and deals with subjects related to the nature, function and use of literacy and the development, learning, and teaching of literacy in early childhood.

The contributions reflect early childhood literacy as a worldwide and social phenomenon, and emphasize the evolution of literacy in relation to changes in contemporary culture and technological innovation.

Contents
PART ONE: PERSPECTIVES ON EARLY CHILDHOOD LITERACY \ Julia Gillen and Nigel Hall The Emergence of Early Childhood Literacy \ Radhika Viruru Postcolonial Perspectives on Childhood and Literacy \ Elaine Millard Gender and Early Childhood Literacy \ Aria Razfar and Kris Gutiérrez Reconceptualizing Early Childhood Literacy: The Sociocultural Influence \ PART TWO: EARLY CHILDHOOD LITERACY IN FAMILIES, COMMUNITIES AND CULTURES \ Michele Knobel and Colin Lankshear Researching Young Children's Out-of-School Literacy Practices \ Patricia Baquedano-Lopez Language, Literacy and Community \ Eve Gregory and Charmian Kenner The Out-of-School Schooling of Literacy \ Trevor H. Cairney Literacy Within Family Life \ Peter Hannon Family Literacy Programmes \ Jackie Marsh Early Childhood Literacy and Popular Culture \ Muriel Robinson and Margaret Mackey Film and Television \ PART THREE: EARLY MOVES IN LITERACY \ Lesley Lancaster Moving into Literacy: How It All Begins \ Gunther Kress Perspectives on Making Meaning : The Differential Principles and Means of Adults and Children \ Gerald Coles Brain Activity, Genetics and Learning to Read \ Charmian Kenner and Eve Gregory Becoming Biliterate \ Carol Fox Playing the Storyteller: Some Principles for Learning Literacy in the Early Years of Schooling \ Roger Beard Uncovering the Key Skills of Reading \ Rhona Stainthorp Phonology and Learning to Read \ Miriam Martinez, Nancy Roser and Caitlin Dooley Young Children's Literacy Meaning Making \ Maria Nikolajeva Verbal and Visual Literacy: The Role of Picturebooks in the Reading Experience of Young Children \ Alan Luke, Victoria Carrington and Cushla Kapitzke Textbooks and Early Childhood Literacy \ Deborah Wells Rowe The Nature of Young Children's Authoring \ Patricia L. Scharer and Jerry Zutell The Development of Spelling \ Frances Christie Writing the World \ PART FOUR: LITERACY IN PRESCHOOL SETTINGS AND SCHOOLS \ Joanne Larson and Shira May Peterson Talk and Discourse in Formal Learning Settings \ Kathy Hall Effective Literacy Teaching in the Early Years of School: A Review of Evidence \ Laurie Makin Creating Positive Literacy Learning Environments in Early Childhood \ Linda D. Labbo and David Reinking Computers and Early Literacy Education \ Barbara Comber Critical Literacy: What Does it Look Like in the Early Years? \ Sharon Murphy Finding Literacy: A Review of Research on Literacy Assessment in Early Childhood \ PART FIVE: RESEARCHING EARLY CHILDHOOD LITERACY \ David Bloome and Laurie Katz Methodologies in Research on Young Children and Literacy \ Jeanette Rhedding-Jones Feminist Methodologies and Research for Early Childhood Literacies \ Brian Cambourne Taking a Naturalistic Viewpoint in Early Childhood Literacy Research

2003 • 464 pages
Cloth (0-7619-7437-7)

P·C·P **Paul Chapman Publishing**
A SAGE Publications Company

⑤SAGE Publications
40 Years 1965-2005